THE MARRIAGE OF FIGARO

Beaumarchais

Adapted by
Richard Nelson

BROADWAY PLAY PUBLISHING INC
224 E 62nd St, NY NY 10065-8201
212 772-8334 fax: 212 772-8358
BroadwayPlayPub.com

THE MARRIAGE OF FIGARO
© Copyright 1991 by Richard Nelson

Cover photo by Joe Giannetti

First printing: December 1991
This edition: September 2016

I S B N: 978-0-88145-099-6

Book design: Marie Donovan
Page make-up: Adobe Indesign
Typeface: Palatino
Printed and bound in the U S A

This adaptation of THE MARRIAGE OF FIGARO was first produced at the Guthrie Theater (Liviu Ciulei, Artistic Director) on 15 July 1982, with the following cast and creative contributors:

COUNT ALMAVIVA	David Warrilow
COUNTESS	Christine Rose
FIGARO	Robert Dorfman
SUZANNE	Jana Schneider
MARCELINE	Catherine Burns
ANTONIO	Fred Applegate
FANCHETTE	Rana Haugen
CHERUBIN	Caitlin Clarke
BARTHOLO	Henry Stram
BAZILE	Richard Ooms
GRIPE-SOLEIL	Fruud Smith
PEDRILLE	Richard Howard
Peasants	Lynn Alexander, Sharon Faye Bialy Hosmer Brown, Kim Green, Curtis Hastings Cecil Lester, John D Mayor, Tamara Nerby Christopher Trotter, Luella St Ville, Dona Werner
Shepherd children	Andrea Bebel, Polly Cohen Elena Giannetti, Linda Roberts

Director	Andrei Serban
Set & costume designer	Beni Montesor
Composer	Richard Peaslee
Dramaturg	Michael Lupu

This adaptation was subsequently produced on
Broadway by Circle in the Square (Theodore Mann,
Artistic Director; Paul Libin, Managing Director) on
10 October 1985 with the following cast and creative
contributors:

COUNT ALMAVIVA ....Christopher Reeve
COUNTESS...Dana Ivey
FIGARO... Anthony Heald
SUZANNE ....Mary Elizabeth Mastrantonio
MARCELINE .... Carol Teitel
ANTONIO...William Duell
FANCHETTE ....Debbie Marrill
CHERUBIN...Caitlin Clarke
BARTHOLO.. Louis Zorich
BAZILE ....James Cahill
GRIPE-SOLEIL ....Dan Nutu
PEDRILLE............... Daniel D Scott, Scott Lindsay Johnson
Peasants ....Robertson Carricart, Francine Forbes
                                        David Giella, Paula Redinger
                                        Connie Roderick, Luke Sickle

Shepherd children............. Edna Harris, Piper Lawrence
                                        Carol-Ann Plante

Director .... Andrei Serban
Designer .... Beni Montresor
Composer ....Richard Peaslee

CHARACTERS

Count Almaviva
Countess, *his wife*
Figaro, *his valet*
Suzanne, Figaro's *fiancée*
Marceline, *housekeeper*
Antonio, *gardener, uncle of* Suzanne, *and father of*
   Fanchette
Fanchette
Cherubin, *a page*
Bartholo, *doctor from Seville*
Bazile, *music teacher*
Gripe-Soleil, *a goat herder*
Pedrille
A Shepherdess
Peasants, workmen, and young girls

ACT ONE

(A half-furnished room. A large armchair center. FIGARO measures the floor with a measuring stick. SUZANNE arranges a small bouquet of orange flowers in her hair. This bouquet is "the bonnet of the bride".)

FIGARO: Nineteen feet by twenty-six.

SUZANNE: Figaro, what do you think?

FIGARO: *(Taking her hand)* To the loving eye of the husband, there can be no sweeter sight than the virginal bonnet upon his bride's lovely head the morning of the wedding.

SUZANNE: *(Pulls back)* What are you measuring?

FIGARO: I'm trying to see if the bed His Lordship's given us fits in here.

SUZANNE: In here?

FIGARO: He's given us this room.

SUZANNE: Give it back to him.

FIGARO: Why?

SUZANNE: I don't like it.

FIGARO: You have a reason?

SUZANNE: Because.

FIGARO: Ah. A typical woman's reason.

SUZANNE: If I were to give you a reason then I would be trying to convince you, but why should I try to convince you when I know I am right?

FIGARO: A typical woman's argument. But tell me what's wrong with this room? It's comfortable. It's convenient. Her Ladyship's room is there; His Lordship's there. Say, Madam wakes up ill in the middle of the night, she rings and in two steps, bang, you're at her side. His Lordship wants me, he tinkles, and in three leaps, bang, I'm there.

SUZANNE: And say he tinkles in the morning, sends you off on a long errand, and in two steps, bang, he's at my door, and in three leaps—!

FIGARO: Bang?!

SUZANNE: Keep calm.

FIGARO: Keep calm about what?

SUZANNE: About this—His Lordship, Count Almaviva, has gotten bored with wooing country girls so he's coming home, not to his wife, but to yours. Now do you understand? And this arrangement here will not exactly harm his plans. And his loyal Bazile, my "noble" singing teacher, has already attempted to procure me for His Lordship while giving me my lesson.

FIGARO: I can't believe it.

SUZANNE: What did you think my dowry was for? To reward your faithful service?

FIGARO: I had hoped as much.

SUZANNE: They say a man with hope is a fool.

FIGARO: I have heard this said.

SUZANNE: There are those who choose not to believe it.

FIGARO: They are wrong.

SUZANNE: Then understand that this dowry is meant as payment for services to be rendered by me, today, sometime, in secret, following the ancient custom and right of noblemen.

FIGARO: A right which His Lordship abolished when he himself married.

SUZANNE: For this he now repents and hopes to redeem himself with your fiancée.

FIGARO: After all I've done for him, he turns and stabs me in the back.

SUZANNE: I don't think it's your back he wants to stab at.

FIGARO: Very funny. There must be some way to catch him. Some scheme to lure him into a snare and trap him—without, of course, us losing the dowry.

SUZANNE: Intrigue and money—you're in your element now.

(A ring from inside)

SUZANNE: Madam's awake. She made me promise that she'd be the first I'd talk to on my wedding day.

FIGARO: For God's sake why?

SUZANNE: There's an old saying that it brings good luck to neglected wives. Think hard about what to do.

FIGARO: A kiss to uncork my thoughts.

SUZANNE: Today you want me to kiss my lover, but tomorrow what would my husband say?

(FIGARO kisses SUZANNE.)

SUZANNE: Stop!

FIGARO: You don't know how much I love you.

SUZANNE: (Pulling away) You tell me so from morning to night.

FIGARO: I'll stop, when I can prove it to you from night to morning.

(SUZANNE *goes.*)

FIGARO: She's so delightful. Always laughing, so full of fun and life. But also well behaved... *(Walks around, rubbing his hands together)* But my Lord. My dear Lord. I wondered why you wanted to take me with you to London as your courier. Now I know. Three promotions in one: You, Sir, gain the rewards of a king's ambassador; I, the thrills of politics; and Suzanne, the respect of a bedroom ministress. While I'm galloping off in one direction, you're tip-toeing in another. While I'm knocking myself out, getting covered in mud for the glory of your family, you are condescending to increase mine. A kind of reciprocity, I suppose. But a bit extreme. —And you, Bazile, I'll teach you how to limp. No. I'll be more clever than that. I'll hide my feelings and play them one against the other. You'll have to stay on your toes today, Figaro. First I'll move up the hour of the wedding, to thwart Marceline who is so crazy for me, then pocket the dowry, put the Count on the wrong scent, show up Bazile, and....

(BARTHOLO *and* MARCELINE *enter.*)

FIGARO: Ah, it's the doctor; the party's now complete! Is it my wedding to Suzanne which brings you to the castle, dear Doctor?

BARTHOLO: *(Distainful)* Of course not.

FIGARO: If it had, I'd have been touched.

BARTHOLO: I doubt it.

FIGARO: Then does some sick mule desire the Doctor's attention?

BARTHOLO: *(Angry)* You have a rabid mouth. Get out.

FIGARO: Offended, Doctor? Men in your profession have no feelings to offend. *(He goes.)* Farewell, Marceline: still pleading your case against me?

BARTHOLO: *(Watching him go)* He hasn't changed one bit.

MARCELINE: Nor have you, Doctor. Still so serious and cold, one could die waiting for your help.

BARTHOLO: So why was I called? Has the Count had an accident?

MARCELINE: No, Doctor.

BARTHOLO: Then what about the Countess, is she ill?

MARCELINE: She wastes away.

BARTHOLO: For what reason?

MARCELINE: The Count neglects her. It is hard to understand him. One minute jealous, the next a libertine.

BARTHOLO: Libertine out of boredom, jealous out of vanity; this is normal.

MARCELINE: Today, for example, he allows our Suzanne to marry his Figaro.

BARTHOLO: A wedding His Lordship has made necessary?

MARCELINE: Not quite. Or not yet, as he does secretly desire to share the bride.

BARTHOLO: Can't he just make a deal with Figaro?

MARCELINE: Bazile says no.

BARTHOLO: What's he doing here?

MARCELINE: As much trouble as he can.

BARTHOLO: This place is a den of thieves.

MARCELINE: The worst of the matter is his boring passion for me.

BARTHOLO: That is easily cured.

MARCELINE: How?

BARTHOLO: By marrying him.

MARCELINE: Then why didn't you cure mine for you in the same way? It was your duty. Don't you ever wonder what's become of our little Emmanuel, the fruit of our passion?

BARTHOLO: *(Taking off his hat)* Did I come from Seville to listen to this nonsense? If you're going to start up again about marrying you....

MARCELINE: I won't bring it up again. But if you won't do your duty and marry me, then at least help me to marry someone else.

BARTHOLO: My pleasure. So tell me: Who is the mortal who has been so forsaken by Heaven and women?

MARCELINE: Who else, Doctor, but the handsome, gay, loveable Figaro!

BARTHOLO: This rogue?

MARCELINE: He never gets angry, he's always in a good mood, he's so carefree, so pleasure-loving, so alive, and generous, oh so generous....

BARTHOLO: Like a thief.

MARCELINE: Like a lord... In one word: charming. But he's such a monster.

BARTHOLO: And his Suzanne?

MARCELINE: With your help, Doctor, she won't get him, no matter how cunning she is. I have something over him.

BARTHOLO: But the wedding's today.

MARCELINE: That's why there isn't much time. I could tell you more, if I weren't so afraid of divulging a little secret women hide.

BARTHOLO: There can be no secret between a woman and her doctor.

MARCELINE: I can keep nothing from you. You see, my sex is ardent but timid. Even the most daring woman, when she finds herself attracted to a pleasure, hears a little voice inside her say: "Be beautiful, if you can, wise if you want, but at all cost be careful". So let's threaten to make public the Count's propositions, and this will alarm Suzanne.

BARTHOLO: So we frighten her, what then?

MARCELINE: Ashamed of being so disgraced, she'll only resist the Count more, and he, in revenge, will support me in opposing this wedding. Thus making mine a certainty.

BARTHOLO: Makes sense.

MARCELINE: How wonderful it will be!

BARTHOLO: To punish the villain!

MARCELINE: To marry him, Doctor, to marry him!

(SUZANNE *enters, carrying a bonnet with a large ribbon in her hands and a dress over her arms.*)

SUZANNE: To marry him! To marry him! Who? My Figaro?

MARCELINE: (*Bitterly*) Why not? You want to, don't you?

BARTHOLO: (*Laughing*) The logic of women when they're angry! We were only saying how lucky he is to have you.

MARCELINE: To say nothing about the Count.

SUZANNE: The jealousy of this Madam is as well known as her claims on Figaro are slight.

MARCELINE: Maybe my claims would seem stronger had I cemented them in the same way as Madam has.

SUZANNE: My ways require intelligence, Madam.

MARCELINE: How pure she is. As innocent as an old judge!

SUZANNE: *(Curtseying)* Your servant, Madam. You have a bitter tongue.

MARCELINE: *(Curtseying)* Madam. The truth is a bitter pill.

(BARTHOLO and MARCELINE go.)

SUZANNE: Good day, witch! Just because she's had a little education and was allowed to torment Her Ladyship's youth, she thinks she can boss everyone around! *(Throws the dress on the chair)* I forgot what I came in for.

(CHERUBIN hurries in.)

CHERUBIN: Suzanne! I've waited two hours to get you alone. Today is your wedding day, and today I must depart!

SUZANNE: How are those two things related?

CHERUBIN: *(Pitifully)* Suzanne, the Count has dismissed me!

SUZANNE: *(Mimicking him)* Cherubin, what have you done?!

CHERUBIN: He caught me yesterday evening in Fanchette's room. I was there helping her rehearse the small role she's to play in your ceremony tonight. He flew into a fury: "Leave," he says to me, "leave you little…" I dare not repeat, in front of a woman, the word he now spoke. "Leave, you will not stay another day in this castle." I don't know what to do. If Her Ladyship, my godmother, does not change his mind, I will never see you again.

SUZANNE: Me? So now it's me? I thought it was Her Ladyship that you pined for.

CHERUBIN: Oh, Suzanne, she is so beautiful and so noble, but she is also so…untouchable.

SUZANNE: Which is to say I am not, and you can dare to hope….

CHERUBIN: You're being mean, you know only too well that I dare not dare. But fortunate you are to see her all the time, to speak with her, to dress her in the morning, to undress her in the night, button by button…. Oh, Suzanne, what I would give…. What's that?

SUZANNE: *(Mimicking him)* `Tis the fortunate bonnet and the fortunate ribbon which ties the fortunate hair of your godmother at night.

CHERUBIN: Her ribbon? I want it.

(SUZANNE pulls it back.)

CHERUBIN: Please, my love, give it to me.

SUZANNE: "Your love"! Who do you think you are, you little brat?

(CHERUBIN snatches the ribbon.)

CHERUBIN: The ribbon! *(Running behind the chair)* Tell her you mislaied it, you ripped it, you lost it. Tell her anything you want.

SUZANNE: *(Going after him)* Are you going to give it back? *(She tries to take it.)*

CHERUBIN: *(Takes a song from his pocket)* Let me go! Here, I'll give you this ballad I wrote; and while in exile from our beautiful Ladyship, with my heart heavy and low, I shall think of you often, and these memories shall be the only ray of joy my heart will know.

SUZANNE: *(Grabs the ballad)* "The only ray of joy!" You little rake. Who do you think you're talking to— Fanchette?! First her, then Her Ladyship, and now me!

CHERUBIN: *(Ecstatic)* Yes, I confess it! Something has happened to me that I don't understand. I find my chest twitching, my heart racing at the mere mention of a woman; the words "love" and "pleasure" stir me and make me shake. The need to say "I love you" to someone has become so urgent, that I say it even when I'm alone walking in the garden. I say it to Her Ladyship, to you, to a tree, the clouds, the wind which floats my words away until they are lost. Yesterday I came across Marceline....

SUZANNE: Marceline! *(Laughs)* Ha ha ha ha!

CHERUBIN: What's wrong? She is a woman. She is a girl! There it is— "Girl"! "Woman"! "Girl" "Woman". Such sweet words, and so provocative!

SUZANNE: He's mad.

CHERUBIN: Fanchette is sweet because she at least listens to me, but not you.

SUZANNE: How sad it must be! *(She tries to take the ribbon.)*

CHERUBIN: *(Pulls back)* Ah! Don't even try! You'd have to kill me first. But if the ballad's not payment enough, I'll throw in a few thousand kisses.

(CHERUBIN chases SUZANNE around.)

SUZANNE: *(Running)* And I'll throw my hand across your face a few thousand times. I'll complain to Her Ladyship; and I'll go to His Lordship and say: "What you have done, Sir, is a very good thing. Throw this little thief from our house, send him back to his parents. He dares to desire to be Madam's lover, and for practice he tries kissing me."

CHERUBIN: *(Seeing the COUNT enter)* I'm dead! *(Hides behind the chair)*

SUZANNE: What's wrong with you? *(Seeing the* COUNT*)* Ah!!! *(She goes to the chair, trying to mask* CHERUBIN.*)*

COUNT: *(Coming closer)* You're moved. You're talking to yourself. Your face is flushed. But not unexpected on a day like today.

SUZANNE: Sir, what do you want? If someone were to find you here with me....

COUNT: That would distress me, yet you know the interest I take in you. Bazile, I believe, has not kept you blind to my love. I have only a moment to tell you my plans. Listen. *(He sits in the chair.)*

SUZANNE: I won't listen!

COUNT: *(Takes her hand)* One word. You know the King has named me his ambassador. I plan to take Figaro with me. It'll be a nice promotion for him. And as it is the duty of a wife to follow her husband....

SUZANNE: If only I had the nerve to speak.

COUNT: *(Pulls her closer)* Speak. Speak, my child. Flex that authority you shall have over me for life.

SUZANNE: *(Frightened)* I can't. I can't. Please, go.

COUNT: You were about to say?

SUZANNE: I forget.

COUNT: Something about a wife's duty.

SUZANNE: Yes. When His Lordship out of love married Her Ladyship he abolished forever a certain custom and right of noblemen....

COUNT: *(Merrily)* A great loss for the girls! Suzanne, what a charming custom it was! Meet me at dusk in the garden, and we can talk about it; and for this small favor, you shall be repaid in kind.

BAZILE: *(Off)* His Lordship's not in his bedroom.

COUNT: *(Standing)* Who's that?

SUZANNE: Just my luck.

COUNT: Go quick, so he doesn't see you.

SUZANNE: And leave you in here?

BAZILE: *(Off, yells)* He was with Her Ladyship. I'll go see.

COUNT: No place to hide! Behind the chair! This won't do for long, get rid of him fast.

(SUZANNE tries to stop him; he gently pushes her away, she throws herself between him and CHERUBIN, but just as the COUNT bends down to take his hiding place, CHERUBIN runs around the chair and throws himself into the chair, kneeling, crouching, and terrified. SUZANNE takes the dress and covers CHERUBIN and stands in front of the chair.)

(BAZILE enters.)

BAZILE: Have you seen His Lordship, Miss?

SUZANNE: *(Sharply)* No. Why would I see him. Leave me alone.

BAZILE: *(Coming closer)* If you were to be a little more reasonable, then my asking would not be surprising. It's Figaro who's looking for him.

SUZANNE: Then he seeks the man who—after you— wishes him the most harm.

COUNT: *(Aside)* Now I'll see how well he serves me.

BAZILE: Is to wish the best for the wife, to wish the worst for the husband?

SUZANNE: Your corrupt mind could never understand such logic.

BAZILE: Because of one silly ceremony, what yesterday was defended is tomorrow given away.

SUZANNE: How dare you!

BAZILE: Of all the serious things, I have often thought marriage to be the most farcical.

SUZANNE: *(Outraged)* How can you? Who told you you could come in here?

BAZILE: There, there, little spitfire. Keep calm. You won't be asked to do anything you don't want to do. But don't expect Figaro to stand up to His Lordship; and without the little page around....

SUZANNE: *(Timidly)* Cherubin?

BAZILE: Your little shadow. Just this morning I saw him prowling around trying to get in here. Is this not true?

SUZANNE: You are an evil person. Get out!

BAZILE: An evil man is simply one who sees the world clearly. And the ballad he was secretly composing, was it for you?

SUZANNE: *(Angry)* Yes, for me!

BAZILE: Or was it for Her Ladyship. Gossip has it that he cannot take his eyes off her. He shouldn't play games there; His Lordship can be brutal.

SUZANNE: *(Outraged)* You scandal monger! How can you slander this poor unfortunate child. He's in enough trouble as it is!

BAZILE: I say only what everyone is saying.

COUNT: *(Standing)* Everyone is saying this?!

SUZANNE: Oh God.

BAZILE: Ah! Ah!

COUNT: Quick, Bazile, I want him thrown out!

BAZILE: I'm sorry I ever came in here.

SUZANNE: Oh God! Oh God!

COUNT: *(To BAZILE)* She's in shock. Sit her in the chair.

SUZANNE: (*Pushes him away*) I don't want to sit. You have no right to come in here.

COUNT: There's two of us, my dear. There's no danger.

BAZILE: I would never have said that about the page if I knew you could hear it.

COUNT: Fifty pistoles, a horse, and a good kick back to his parents.

BAZILE: Because of a joke, Sir?

COUNT: The little lech. I caught him again yesterday with the gardener's daughter.

BAZILE: With Fanchette?

COUNT: And in her room.

SUZANNE: (*Angry*) Where His Lordship himself was headed!

COUNT: (*Cheerily*) That's a thought.

BAZILE: She's probably right.

COUNT: No, I was looking for our drunken gardener, Antonio. I knock; then after a long pause, the door opens, your cousin looks worried, I become suspicious, I talk to her and at the same time I investigate. Behind the door there is a piece of cloth, like a curtain, hanging on a coat stand. I appear not to notice while I gently, very gently raise His cloth... (*To demonstrate he raises the dress on the chair.*) ...and I find.... (*Sees* CHERUBIN) Ah!

BAZILE: Ah! Ah!

COUNT: This is just like last night.

BAZILE: Even better.

COUNT: I confess I am shocked, Miss. Is this how you prepare yourself for marriage? Was it to receive my page that you desired to be alone? And you, Sir, you appear unable to control yourself. Your abominable conduct now extends to not only offending Her Ladyship, whose servant this girl is, but to your friend, whose wife this girl is soon to be! I will not stand idly by and see Figaro, a man I esteem, be made the victim by such a fraud as yourself! Bazile, where is Figaro?

SUZANNE: *(Outraged)* There is no fraud and no victim! He was right here all the time you were talking to me.

COUNT: That better be a lie; his worst enemy could not wish him worse luck.

SUZANNE: He was here begging me to get him forgiven. When you came in, he got scared, and hid behind this chair.

COUNT: Liar! I sat there when I came in.

CHERUBIN: And I was trembling behind you.

COUNT: Another lie! I hid there myself.

CHERUBIN: Excuse me, Sir, but that is when I squatted in the chair.

COUNT: *(Angry)* Then this snake has heard us!

CHERUBIN: On the contrary, Sir, I made like this. *(Covers his ears)*

COUNT: Liars! *(To* SUZANNE*)* You can forget about marrying Figaro!

BAZILE: Calm down, someone's coming.

*(*COUNTESS, FIGARO, *and* FANCHETTE *enter with many servants and peasants who are all dressed in white.* FIGARO *carries a woman's bonnet which is garnished with white feathers and ribbons.)*

FIGARO: *(To* COUNTESS*)* Only you, Madam, can obtain for us this favor.

COUNTESS: *(To* COUNT*)* You see, Sir, how they assume an influence which I do not possess; however, as their request is not unreasonable....

COUNT: *(Embarrassed)* It would have to be more than just that....

FIGARO: *(Aside to* SUZANNE*)* Help me out.

SUZANNE: *(Aside to* FIGARO*)* It's hopeless.

FIGARO: *(Aside to* SUZANNE*)* Try.

COUNT: *(To* FIGARO*)* What is it you want?

FIGARO: Your Lordship, your vassals, in great appreciation for your abolishment of a certain loathsome custom, which in your love for Madam....

COUNT: Yes, this custom no longer exists; now get to the point.

FIGARO: *(Slyly)* It is felt that this would be a good time to acclaim the virtue of so good a master. And as I shall be the first to benefit from your act, I would like my wedding today to be a celebration of it.

COUNT: *(Embarrassed)* You must be joking.

FIGARO: *(Taking* SUZANNE *by the hand)* Permit this young creature, whose honor your wisdom has preserved, to receive publicly from your hand this virginal bonnet. Let this act symbolize the purity of your intentions and become a new custom to be celebrated at all weddings.

COUNT: *(Embarrassed)* It is really not necessary.

FIGARO: Join me, friends!

EVERYONE: HIS LORDSHIP! HIS LORDSHIP!

SUZANNE: *(To* COUNT*)* It's only what you deserve.

COUNT: *(Aside)* Traitoress.

FIGARO: Look at her, Sir. No more beautiful fiancée could better express the grandeur of your sacrifice.

SUZANNE: Leave me out of this, just praise him.

COUNT: *(Aside)* What a joke.

COUNTESS: I couple my thanks to theirs, Sir, and shall forever cherish this new custom as it is an expression of the love you have had for me.

COUNT: And always shall, Madam. It is to this love that I yield.

EVERYONE: HURRAH! BRAVO!

COUNT: *(Aside)* I've been had. *(Aloud)* But I ask only that we postpone this ceremony a little so we can better prepare ourselves for it. *(Aside)* Quick, let's find Marceline.

FIGARO: *(To* CHERUBIN*)* And you, runt, why aren't you cheering?

SUZANNE: He's in despair; His Lordship is sending him away.

COUNTESS: Then, I ask for his pardon.

COUNT: He hasn't deserved it.

COUNTESS: But he's so young!

COUNT: Not as young as you think.

CHERUBIN: *(Trembling)* The right to be generous and pardon was not the one you renounced when you married Her Ladyship.

COUNTESS: He renounced only that right which you found loathsome.

COUNT: Enough! It seems that everyone wants him pardoned, so he is. And I'll do more than that: I shall give him his own company in my regiment.

EVERYONE: HURRAH! BRAVO!

COUNT: On the condition that he leave immediately to join it in Catalonia.

FIGARO: Let him stay until tomorrow.

COUNT: No.

CHERUBIN: I will obey.

COUNT: Approach your sponsor and ask for her protection.

(CHERUBIN *kneels in front of the* COUNTESS, *but cannot speak.*)

COUNTESS: (*Affected*) Since one cannot keep you even for one day, go, young man. A new life calls. Go perform with dignity, honor us, remember this house, where your youth has been so indulged. Be obedient, honorable, brave; we will rejoice in your success.

(CHERUBIN *stands and returns to his place.*)

COUNT: You are moved, Madam.

COUNTESS: I won't deny it. Who knows what lies before a youth thrown into a career so full of danger.

COUNT: (*Aside*) Bazile was right! (*Aloud*) Young man, embrace Suzanne for the last time.

FIGARO: What do you mean, Sir? He'll still be spending winters here. Embrace me too, Captain!

(*They embrace.*)

FIGARO: Goodbye, my little Cherubin. It will be a very different life, my child. No more skulking around women's bedrooms, no more rich pastries and afternoon teas, nor games or sports or summer play. Dammit, just hearty soldiers, weathered and worse for wear, with heavy muskets weighing 'em down. Turn to the right, turn to the left, and forward march into glory! And no stumbling, unless there's a big blast from a cannon....

SUZANNE: Stop it!

COUNTESS: What a prediction!

COUNT: Where's Marceline? Why isn't she with the rest of you?

FANCHETTE: Sir, she's on her way to town. I saw her go down the path by the farm with the doctor.

COUNT: *(Quickly)* He's here?

BAZILE: She grabbed him the moment he walked in.

COUNT: *(Aside)* He couldn't have come at a better time.

FIGARO: Frustrated in love, she wanted to frustrate our ceremony.

COUNT: *(Aside)* She will. I promise you.

FANCHETTE: Your Lordship, have we been pardoned for yesterday?

COUNT: Yes. Yes, of course. Let us go, Madam. Bazile, stop by my room.

SUZANNE: *(To FIGARO)* You'll come back to me?

FIGARO: *(Whispers to SUZANNE)* Has he sniffed the bait?

SUZANNE: *(Whispers)* Silly boy!

(As they all exit except CHERUBIN, FIGARO, and SUZANNE.)

FIGARO: This act's been completed, the rest of the show follows tonight. Just keep in mind that we must not be like some actors who never perform as badly as when the critics are in the house. Tomorrow, there can be no excuses. We must know our roles well.

CHERUBIN: Aren't you forgetting that I have to leave?

FIGARO: And you, of course, want to stay.

CHERUBIN: If only I could!

FIGARO: If we're clever, you can. Quit sulking and get set to leave. Put on your coat, pack your bags, and make sure this is seen. Ride to the gate, wave goodbye, then gallop as far as the farm, there unmount and return on foot by the back way. His Lordship will think you've left so keep out of his sight. Tomorrow I'll try to change his mind.

CHERUBIN: But Fanchette doesn't know her role!

SUZANNE: Then what have you been doing with her for the last eight days?

FIGARO: You have nothing else to do today, rehearse her.

SUZANNE: But be careful. Her father's already suspicious, he's beaten her once. And you know what they say, Cherubin: "Too much rehearsal..."

FIGARO: "Too much rehearsal..." what?

SUZANNE: Spoils your performance!

(They laugh.)

FIGARO: Very good. Very good.

END ACT ONE

ACT TWO

(A bedroom. The main door right; a closet door left. Door to the maid's room, upstage. A window on the opposite side.)

(COUNTESS and SUZANNE enter from the main door.)

COUNTESS: *(Throwing herself in a chair)* Close the door, Suzanne. I want to know it all.

SUZANNE: You know I tell you everything.

COUNTESS: Then he tried to seduce you?

SUZANNE: I wouldn't say that. His Lordship wouldn't go to that much trouble over a servant. He wanted to buy me.

COUNTESS: And the little page was there?

SUZANNE: Hiding behind the chair. He came to plead for your mercy.

COUNTESS: Why didn't he come to me? Did he think I'd refuse?

SUZANNE: That's what I said. But he was in such pain at having to leave you. "Oh Suzanne, she is so beautiful, so noble, but she is also so…untouchable."

COUNTESS: Is that how he sees me? After all this time?

SUZANNE: Then he saw your ribbon and he grabbed it.

COUNTESS: My ribbon? How childish.

SUZANNE: I tried to take it from him. But, Madam, he was like a lion, his eyes all aglow.

COUNTESS: *(Dreamily)* These are just a child's follies. How did you leave it with my husband?

SUZANNE: That if I chose not to understand his wishes, he would support Marceline and her cause.

COUNTESS: *(Getting up and briskly fanning herself)* He loves me—no more.

SUZANNE: Then why would he be jealous?

COUNTESS: Like all husbands, my dear, out of vanity. I loved him too much; I wearied him with affection, tired him with my love. This has been my only mistake. For this you have told me, my dear, I take no offense. You shall marry Figaro. Only he can help us now. When is he coming?

SUZANNE: As soon as the hunt gets started.

COUNTESS: *(Fanning herself)* Open the window a little. It's hot in here.

SUZANNE: You've been walking and talking so passionately you've made yourself hot.

COUNTESS: *(Still dreaming)* He tries so hard to avoid me…. Men are despicable.

SUZANNE: *(At the window)* His Lordship is riding across the garden. Pedrille's with him, followed by two, three, four dogs.

COUNTESS: That'll give us time. *(She sits.)* Is someone knocking, Suzanne?

SUZANNE: *(Hurrying to open the door, singing)* It's my Figaro! It's my Figaro! *(At the door)* Come in. Madam is anxious to see you.

(FIGARO enters.)

FIGARO: And how about you? Madam, there is nothing to worry about. A mere trifle, if anything. The Count finds a young wife attractive and wishes to make her his mistress. It's all quite natural.

SUZANNE: Natural?

FIGARO: I'm to be attached to the embassy, and Suzanne attached to the ambassador.

SUZANNE: Are you done?

FIGARO: And because my fiancée, Suzanne, chooses not to accept this commission, he will graduate Marceline by taking up her cause. What could be simpler? Hurt those who hurt us. Everybody does that. And so have we. All it took was one slight insinuation about you, Madam....

COUNTESS: A man as jealous as he is!

FIGARO: So much the better. With men of his character, it doesn't take much to get their blood boiling. And once they're thoroughly crazed, you can lead them by the nose wherever you want, even over a cliff. But why am I telling you this? You women do this all the time. I've sent Bazile an anonymous letter, warning His Lordship that a certain young man shall be trying to see you tonight at the ceremony.

COUNTESS: So it is my honor that you are playing with.

FIGARO: There are few women, Madam, whose honor I would dare play with, without fearing that the woman had played with it herself.

COUNTESS: So I'm to be thankful to you for that?

FIGARO: Think of it in this way. We have simply rescheduled his day. The time he'd set aside to enjoy my wife, he now spends worrying about what his own might enjoy. He's already beside himself. He's out there now galloping around in circles. Just send word to His Lordship that you'll meet him at dusk in the garden.

SUZANNE: So that's your whole plan?

FIGARO: My dear woman, just let me finish. People who only criticize everything never do anything, achieve nothing, and are good for nothing. That's my motto.

SUZANNE: Very pretty.

COUNTESS: You'll let her meet him?

FIGARO: Of course not. I'll send someone else in Suzanne's clothes. And at the rendezvous, we surprise him, and let's just see how the Count gets out of that.

SUZANNE: Who'll wear my clothes?

FIGARO: Cherubin.

COUNTESS: He's gone.

FIGARO: We'll see. Just trust me.

SUZANNE: We should. When it comes to intrigue, he's had a lot of practice.

FIGARO: I should have been born a courtier.

SUZANNE: They say it's not an easy life.

FIGARO: Receive, take, ask—that's the trick in three words.

COUNTESS: He's so sure of himself, he's got me believing him.

FIGARO: That's the idea.

SUZANNE: So now what?

FIGARO: While His Lordship's away, I'll send in Cherubin. Fix his hair, dress him up. I'll lock him away and rehearse him. And then—Your Lordship—dance! (*He exits.*)

COUNTESS: (*Taking her powder*) Look at me, Suzanne. And that young man will be here any minute.

SUZANNE: Madam doesn't mean to discourage him?

COUNTESS: *(Dreaming, in front of a little mirror)* Of course. Wait till you see how I scold him.

SUZANNE: Let's make him sing his ballad.

(SUZANNE gives ballad to COUNTESS)

COUNTESS: Just look at this hair.

SUZANNE: *(Laughing)* With it combed you'll be able to scold him even better?

COUNTESS: *(Dreaming)* What did you say, Miss?

(A knock on the door)

SUZANNE: Come in, mister captain, we're here.

(CHERUBIN enters.)

CHERUBIN: *(Trembling)* Don't use that word, it just reminds me that I have to leave this place...and a godmother who is so...good!

SUZANNE: And so beautiful!

CHERUBIN: *(With a sigh)* Yes!

SUZANNE: *(Mimicking him)* "Yes. Yes." Such a nice young man and so two-faced. Come on brown eyes, sing your ballad to Madam.

COUNTESS: *(Unfolding it)* Who's it about?

SUZANNE: Look. He's blushing.

CHERUBIN: Is there a law against...loving....

SUZANNE: *(Shoves her fist under his nose)* I'll tell her everything, you runt.

COUNTESS: Will he sing?

CHERUBIN: But, Madam, I'm shaking.

SUZANNE: *(Laughing)* Gnian gnian gnian gnian gnian. The stage is finally set and the author gets cold feet. I'll accompany him.

COUNTESS: Take my guitar.

(COUNTESS *sits on the couch, holding the paper and following the song.* SUZANNE *is behind, reading the music over her shoulder.* CHERUBIN *stands before the* COUNTESS, *his eyes lowered. This tableau is a copy of Vanloo's* The Spanish Conversation.)

CHERUBIN: *(Sings)*
With my charger in the rain
(My heart, my heart has pain)
I roam from plain to plain
Where'er my horse he goes.

Where'er my horse he goes
I carry with me my woes
Down a country lane
(My heart, my heart has pain)
My sponsor I can't gain
My tears run to my toes.

My tears run to my toes
Weighted down by woes
I carve a tree with cane
(My heart, my heart has pain)
Her name will there remain;
The Queen down the road she goes.

The Queen down the road she goes
With her friends and not her foes
To speak to me she deigns
(My heart, my heart has pains)
"What's made you so insane?"
That I'm sad the Queen she knows.

That I'm sad the Queen she knows
All but the reason shows
My Lady and Sovereign
(My heart, my heart has pain)
My love's across that plain
I love her smile and nose.

I love her smile and nose,
I'll kill myself with blows,

The Queen she says refrain
heart, *(My heart has pain)*
And with her I should remain
To follow where'er she goes.

To follow where'er she goes
As her page is how I'll go
I meet the young Helaine,
(My heart, my heart has pain)
Daughter of captain
That she likes me it does show.

SUZANNE: Enough! Enough!

COUNTESS: There is innocence in it—even feeling.

SUZANNE: *(Putting the guitar on the chair)* When it comes to feeling, he's your man. But, Mister Captain, you haven't been told how we wish to liven up the party tonight. Do you know, off hand, if any of my dresses will fit you?

COUNTESS: I doubt it.

SUZANNE: *(Measuring herself against him)* We're about the same size. Let's take off your coat. *(She takes it off.)*

COUNTESS: And if someone comes in?

SUZANNE: Are we doing anything wrong?… I'll close the door. *(Runs and closes it)* It's the hair that I'm most worried about.

COUNTESS: There's a bonnet on my dressing table.

(SUZANNE goes out.)

COUNTESS: The Count won't know you're still here until the ball. We'll tell him, then, it was while you were waiting for your orders that we got this idea.

CHERUBIN: (*Showing the orders*) But I have them. Bazile gave them to me.

COUNTESS: Already? They didn't waste a minute. (*She reads.*) They were in such a hurry they forgot to put a seal on them. (*Hands them back to him*)

SUZANNE: (*Entering with a large bonnet*) A seal? What seal?

COUNTESS: On his orders.

SUZANNE: Already!

COUNTESS: That's what I said. Is that my bonnet?

SUZANNE: (*Sitting by the* COUNTESS) It's the most beautiful one you have. (*She sings with pins in her mouth.*)
Turn around and stop right there
la la la
Handsome captain young and fair
la la la"
(*Fixes his hair*) Madam, he looks delightful!

COUNTESS: Fix his collar, so he looks more feminine.

SUZANNE: (*Fixing it*) There. What do you know, the little brat's become a pretty girl. I think I'm jealous of him. (*Takes him by the chin*) If only we were as pretty.

COUNTESS: You're being silly. Raise his sleeve a little.

(SUZANNE *does*)

COUNTESS: Is that a ribbon on his arm?

SUZANNE: One of yours. I was hoping you'd notice.

COUNTESS: There's blood on it! (*She takes the ribbon off.*)

CHERUBIN: (*Embarrassed*) This morning, getting set to leave, I was harnessing my horse. It jerked its head and the bit scratched my arm.

COUNTESS: And you used a ribbon to....

SUZANNE: A stolen ribbon no less. His arm's so white. Just like a woman's—whiter even than mine. *(Compares her arm)* See?

COUNTESS: If there isn't anything else you want to compare, go get the medicine.

(SUZANNE shoves his head and laughs. He falls on his hands. She goes.)

CHERUBIN: *(Kneeling with his eyes lowered)* The ribbon I had was all the medicine I needed. You will have the ribbon, and I'll be gone and have nothing.

COUNTESS: You won't be gone forever.

CHERUBIN: I'm so unhappy.

COUNTESS: *(Touched)* He's crying. It's Figaro's fault, he shouldn't have said that about soldiers.

CHERUBIN: No. What he said only gave me hope. Because maybe at the moment of my death, my mouth will dare to....

COUNTESS: *(Interrupting him. She dries his eyes with a handkerchief.)* Hush, my child. You're talking nonsense now.

(Knock at the door)

COUNTESS: Who's there?

COUNT: *(Off)* Why is your door locked?

COUNTESS: *(Worried, gets up)* It's my husband! Oh my God!

(To CHERUBIN, who jumps up:)

COUNTESS: No coat. No collar. No sleeves. Alone with me. The room's a mess. The letter's delivered. And he's so jealous.

COUNT: Why don't you open the door?

COUNTESS: I'm...I'm alone.

COUNT: Alone! Then who are you talking to?

COUNTESS: *(Desperately)* To you, of course.

CHERUBIN: *(Aside)* First last night, then this morning, now this. He'll kill me. The closet! *(Runs to the closet, gets in, and closes the door behind him)*

(COUNTESS grabs the key and runs and opens the door.)

COUNTESS: What were we thinking of! What were we thinking of!

(COUNT enters.)

COUNT: I've never known you to lock yourself in before.

COUNTESS: I…I was sorting through my wardrobe with Suzanne. She was here just a minute ago.

COUNT: You seem somehow changed.

COUNTESS: That's not surprising. We were talking about you and she left. Like I said.

COUNT: About me? I came back because I was thinking about you. Getting on my horse, I was handed a letter, the content of which I refuse to believe, though I'll admit to being bothered by it.

COUNTESS: How, Sir? What letter?

COUNT: We are surrounded, Madam, by wicked people. This letter attempted to warn me that a certain person, whom I believed to be gone, planned to contact you today.

COUNTESS: To do so, he'd have to be audacious enough to break down that door, because I have no plans to leave my room at all today.

COUNT: Not even for Suzanne's wedding?

COUNTESS: For nothing in the world. I don't feel well.

COUNT: Fortunately the doctor is here.

(CHERUBIN *knocks a chair over in the closet.*)

COUNT: What's that?

COUNTESS: What's what?

COUNT: That noise.

COUNTESS: I didn't hear anything.

COUNT: Who's in the closet, Madam?

COUNTESS: Why would anybody be in a closet?

COUNT: That's what I'm asking you. I just got here.

COUNTESS: It...it must be Suzanne putting things away.

COUNT: You said she went to her room.

COUNTESS: Or in there. It's not my job to keep track of Suzanne.

COUNT: If it's her, why do you look so worried?

COUNTESS: You mean, why am I worried about my maid?

COUNT: I doubt if it's her you are really worried about.

COUNTESS: If not, maybe I should be, to match the obsession you have for her.

COUNT: *(Angry)* I'm so obsessed with her that I wish to see her this second!

COUNTESS: A wish, I fear, you have made often. I assure you that your suspicions are groundless....

(SUZANNE *enters with clothes.*)

COUNT: The easier then for you to prove them wrong. *(He speaks into the closet.)* Come out of there, Suzanne! That's an order!

(SUZANNE *stops near the alcove.*)

COUNTESS: She's nearly naked, Sir. Is there no place where a woman can be alone? I gave her some clothes as a wedding present and she was trying them on. She ran out when she heard you.

COUNT: If she's so afraid to show herself, then at least she can speak. *(He turns toward the closet.)* Answer me, Suzanne. Are you in the closet?

*(*SUZANNE *throws herself into the alcove and hides.)*

COUNTESS: *(Turns toward the closet; quickly)* Suzanne, I forbid you to answer him. *(To the* COUNT*)* Even tyranny has its limits.

COUNT: *(Moving toward the closet)* Dressed or undressed, if she won't talk, I'll see her.

COUNTESS: *(Stepping in front of him)* If we were any other place, I couldn't stop you, but this is my room!

COUNT: I won't waste my breath asking for the key. It won't take much to take apart this door. Hello! Who ever you are!

COUNTESS: You want to make a scene and attract the whole castle? You'll look like a fool.

COUNT: I can do without your comments, thank you. I need some tools from my room. *(He starts to go out, stops.)* But just to make sure everything remains as it now is, perhaps you will deign to accompany me—in silence of course, I know how much you dislike scenes. Or do I ask too much?

COUNTESS: Who can refuse you anything?

COUNT: Wait, I almost forgot the door to your maid's room. I'll lock it as well. Let there not be even the shadow of a doubt. *(Locks that door)*

COUNTESS: *(Aside)* Really, what were we thinking of!

COUNT: *(Returning to her)* Madam, my arm.

*(*COUNTESS *takes* COUNT's *arm. He raises his voice:)*

COUNT: And as for the Suzanne in the closet, I would be much obliged if she were kind enough to stay in there, as any effort to leave now would only compound her fate.

COUNTESS: Sir, this is an odious adventure.

(COUNT leads COUNTESS out, and locks the door.)

(SUZANNE leaves the alcove, goes to the closet, speaks through the keyhole.)

SUZANNE: Cherubin, open up. Quick, it's me, Suzanne! Quick, get out!

CHERUBIN: *(Coming out)* Oh Suzanne, what a nightmare!

SUZANNE: Get out of here fast!

CHERUBIN: How?

SUZANNE: I don't know. Just get out.

CHERUBIN: And if there's no way out?

SUZANNE: You heard him, he'll strangle you. Run and tell Figaro.

CHERUBIN: Maybe the window.

(They run to it.)

SUZANNE: It's too high. You'd never make it.

CHERUBIN: *(Comes back to her)* The vegetable patch is below. So what if I squash a squash or two.

SUZANNE: *(Holding him back and crying)* He's going to kill himself!

CHERUBIN: Let me jump into the fiery pit! Better to jump than to cause her harm! For luck—I'll take a kiss. *(He kisses her and runs and jumps out the window.)*

SUZANNE: Ah! *(Sinking, she sits for a moment. With great pain she goes to the window and comes back.)* He's already half way down the path! That little pipsqueak, he's as nimble as he's pretty. He won't lack for women. Now to take his place. *(Gets into closet)* Go ahead, Your Lordship, break down the door, if that sort of thing amuses you. I'm not going to say a word. *(Closes herself in)*

(COUNT and COUNTESS return. He carries pliers which he throws on the chair.)

COUNT: Everything is just as I left it. Before breaking the door, I'll ask you one more time: will you open it?

COUNTESS: Were it love which incites this offensive madness, this I could forgive. But can it be that vanity drives you to this excess!

COUNT: Whether love or vanity, you will open this door!

COUNTESS: *(Between him and the door)* Please stop. Look at me—could I be so lacking in self-respect?

COUNT: I'll look inside first and then tell you.

COUNTESS: *(Frightened)* Then you'll see.

COUNT: That it's not Suzanne?

COUNTESS: *(Timidly)* Nor is it any person who should cause you concern. We meant it only as a joke, an innocent joke for tonight. And I swear to you....

COUNT: Swear what?

COUNTESS: That neither I nor he meant to offend you.

COUNT: He! Then it's a man!

COUNTESS: A child!

COUNT: Who?

COUNTESS: I'd rather not name names.

COUNT: I'll kill him!

COUNTESS: Oh God no!

COUNT: Then tell me!

COUNTESS: It's Cherubin.

COUNT: Cherubin! My suspicions and the letter are proved true. *(Beside himself)* Get out of there you little wretch!

COUNTESS: *(Taking him by the waist and pushing him)* Let me explain. Let me explain. He's a little undressed....

COUNT: Undressed!

COUNTESS: He'd taken his vest and coat off, and his sleeves and collar, and he has one of my bonnets on....

COUNT: You worthless woman!

COUNTESS: He has done nothing wrong.

COUNT: *(Furious)* What gall you have to plead for another.

COUNTESS: I will give you the key. But in the name of our love...

COUNT: What love?! *(Taking the key)*

COUNTESS: *(Throwing herself into the chair, she puts a handkerchief to her eyes.)* Oh God, he's going to die.

COUNT: *(Opens the door, recoils)* It's Suzanne!

SUZANNE: *(Coming out laughing)* I will kill him. I will kill him. So why don't you kill the nasty page?

(The COUNT enters the closet.)

(SUZANNE rushes to the COUNTESS.)

SUZANNE: He got away. He jumped.

COUNTESS: I can't move.

(COUNT comes out of the closet. He looks confused.)

(Pause)

COUNT: There's no one there. Was I so totally wrong? Madam, you play comedy very well.

SUZANNE: *(Gaily)* And what about me, Sir?

(COUNTESS, *with her handkerchief over her mouth, says nothing.*)

COUNT: *(Approaching her)* Then it was all a joke, Madam?

COUNTESS: *(Recovering a little)* Of course.

COUNT: A cruel joke. Why?

COUNTESS: Do your actions deserve my pity?

COUNT: I acted as a man of honor must.

COUNTESS: *(Gaining confidence)* Is it honor as well that makes you neglect me?

COUNT: Will you spare me nothing, Madam?

SUZANNE: Admit it, Sir, you deserve it. A little.

COUNT: Rosine!

COUNTESS: I an no longer her that you so loved. I am the Countess Almaviva, the sad abandoned wife you love no more. I plan, Sir, to retire to a nunnery.

SUZANNE: Madam!

COUNT: *(Pleasing)* For pity's sake…

COUNTESS: Where has been your pity for me?

COUNT: But that letter?

COUNTESS: It did not have my consent.

COUNT: Then you knew about it?

COUNTESS: It was Figaro…

COUNT: He's in on this?

COUNTESS: …who gave it to Bazile.

COUNT: Who told me he got it from a peasant. He'll pay for that!

COUNTESS: You ask to be forgiven, while refusing to forgive. That's a man. Say one day I forgave you—on the grounds that the letter provoked you—I would do so only if everyone else was pardoned as well.

COUNT: With all my heart, Madam, I agree. Will I ever be able to make this up to you?

COUNTESS: *(Getting up)* We were both to blame.

COUNT: No, Madam. Only me. But what amazes me most is how you women, in a second, put on such convincing fronts. I saw you blush, you cried, you looked so worried...in fact, you still do.

COUNTESS: *(Forcing a smile)* Your suspicions made me blush. Maybe men aren't sensitive enough to distinguish between a woman's indignation and her guilt.

COUNT: Say again that you forgive me.

COUNTESS: Did I say such a thing, Suzanne?

SUZANNE: I didn't hear it.

COUNT: Then let the word come out.

COUNTESS: Do you think you deserve it, you ingrate?

COUNT: Yes, because I repent.

SUZANNE: To have suspected there was a man in Madam's closet!

COUNT: I have been punished enough....

SUZANNE: To have accused her of lying when she said it was her own maid!

COUNT: Rosine, are you so rigid? Unmoveable?

COUNTESS: Suzanne, I am too weak. What a bad example I am for you. *(Holds the* COUNT's *hand)* Never again will a woman's anger be believed.

SUZANNE: I wouldn't worry, Madam. It's always this way with men.

*(*COUNT *ardently kisses his wife's hand.)*

(FIGARO *enters, out of breath.*)

FIGARO: I heard that the Countess was distressed, so I came as fast as I could…. But I'm pleased to see that I heard wrong.

COUNT: *(Dryly)* You are very attentive.

FIGARO: That's my job. Come along, Suzanne, there are some peasants downstairs with pipes and violins who want to entertain us on our wedding day.

COUNT: But who's going to stay with the Countess?

FIGARO: Is she sick?

COUNT: No. But what about a certain young man who shall be trying to see her tonight?

FIGARO: What young man?

COUNT: The one mentioned in the letter you gave to Bazile.

FIGARO: Who told you that?

SUZANNE: Save your breath, Figaro, we told him everything. That it was you who wrote the letter which had His Lordship believing that it was the page who was in the closet, when actually it was me.

FIGARO: Oh, that.

COUNT: Now what do you have to say for yourself?

COUNTESS: There's no point in hiding anything, Figaro. The joke's over.

FIGARO: *(Searching)* The joke? It's over…? I wish I could say the same about my wedding.

COUNTESS: Let's go, Sir, they're dying to be united. A natural impatience. Come, let's begin their ceremony.

COUNT: *(Aside)* Where the hell is Marceline? *(Aloud)* I have to get dressed first.

COUNTESS: For servants? Why bother?

(ANTONIO *enters, half drunk, holding a smashed vegetable.*)

ANTONIO: My Lord!

COUNT: What is it, Antonio?

ANTONIO: Put bars across the windows. All kinds of things are being thrown out—just a moment ago it was a man.

COUNT: From these windows?

ANTONIO: Look what he did to my vegetables.

SUZANNE: *(Whispers to* FIGARO*)* Watch out, Figaro.

FIGARO: He's been drunk since this morning.

ANTONIO: Since last night.

COUNT: *(Eyes ablaze)* And that man, where is he?!

ANTONIO: You want to know?

SUZANNE: *(To* FIGARO*)* Change the subject, quick!

FIGARO: *(To* ANTONIO*)* Do you always drink?

ANTONIO: If I didn't I'd go mad.

COUNTESS: But to take a drink even when you're not thirsty....

ANTONIO: Madam, to drink without thirst, and to make love all the time, is the only thing that separates us from the rest of the animals.

COUNT: Either tell me what you know or I'll have you thrown out into the street!

ANTONIO: Who says I'd go?

COUNT: *(Shaking him)* You said someone threw a man from that window?

ANTONIO: Yes, Sir. He goes—plop! I would have run after him, but I got my finger stuck in the gate. *(Holds up his finger)* Look at it. It's little head won't move and it's feet don't budge.

COUNT: Would you recognize him?

ANTONIO: I would recognize him, if I had seen him.

SUZANNE: *(To* FIGARO*)* He didn't see him!

FIGARO: Sir, it was I who jumped.

COUNT: You?

ANTONIO: You must have grown a lot in the last few minutes.

FIGARO: When you jump, you curl up. I was waiting for Suzanne in her room. Then I heard you, Sir, and this great commotion. And I got scared that you'd found out I'd written the letter, so I jumped. I even sprained my ankle a little. *(Stamps his foot)*

ANTONIO: Then I should give you back this satchel you dropped.

COUNT: *(Jumps in front of him)* Give me that. *(Opens the satchel, looks at some papers, and closes it)*

FIGARO: *(Aside)* Caught!

COUNT: *(To* FIGARO*)* Tell me what this is.

FIGARO: *(Digging into his pockets, taking out some papers)* Let's see. What could I have dropped?

*(*COUNT *reopens his paper.)*

COUNTESS: *(To* SUZANNE*)* It's his orders!

SUZANNE: It's the orders.

FIGARO: It's that child's orders, of course. He gave them to me and I forgot to give them back. I better run....

COUNT: Why did he give them to you?

FIGARO: *(Embarrassed)* Because...he...needed someone...to do something...to them.

COUNT: *(Looking over the papers)* Needed who to do what?

COUNTESS: *(Whispers to* SUZANNE*)* The seal.

SUZANNE: *(Whispers to* FIGARO*)* There's no seal.

COUNT: *(To* FIGARO*)* You're not answering.

FIGARO: It's nothing major. It's just that it is customary.

COUNT: Customary for what?

FIGARO: For your seal to be fixed to such papers. It probably wasn't worth the bother.

COUNT: *(Reopens the paper and crumples it in anger)* I can see I'm to learn nothing here. *(Aside)* Sooner or later this Figaro will get what's coming to him. *(He makes to leave.)*

FIGARO: *(Stopping him)* Then our wedding, Sir, you'll give us your permission?

*(*BAZILE *enters.)*

BAZILE: Sir, your horse, should I take it back to the stables?

COUNT: *(Aside)* Ah, my "friend" with the letter. *(Aloud)* Bazile, my trusty agent, I have an errand for you.

BAZILE: I an your servant, Sir.

COUNT: Bring me that peasant who gave you the letter. *(He starts to go.)*

BAZILE: Sir, I'm not sure I'd recognize him.

COUNT: You refuse?

BAZILE: No, Sir.

*(*COUNT *leaves.)*

BAZILE: But to me, these peasants all look alike!

FIGARO: Come along, Bazile, I'll sing to you to get you going

BAZILE: But…?

FIGARO: Something light for my fiancée.

(FIGARO *sings as he,* BAZILE, *and* ANTONIO *exit.*)

FIGARO:
Instead of gold
I'd rather be told
I have Suzanne
zan zan zan
zan zan zan
zan zan zan
zan zan zan

To be so bold
Let me unfold
That I'm her man
an an an
an an an
an an an
an an an

(The noise dies away; we do not hear the rest.)

SUZANNE: Oh, Madam, if you could have seen your face when I came out of the closet.

COUNTESS: He really jumped out the window?

SUZANNE: Just up and out, like a bumble bee.

COUNTESS: God help us if my husband finds that child in the castle.

SUZANNE: I'll make sure he's well hidden.

COUNTESS: I wouldn't dare send him to the garden now.

SUZANNE: Well I'm certainly not going. And there goes my marriage again....

COUNTESS: *(Getting up)* Wait. What if instead of him, or you, I went myself?

SUZANNE: You, Madam?

COUNTESS: Then no one could be hurt. And my husband wouldn't have a prayer.... We made it this far, why not keep going? Quick, tell him you'll meet him in the garden. But tell no one else.

SUZANNE: But Figaro?

COUNTESS: No. He'll only complicate it. I'm going on the terrace to ponder about this.

(SUZANNE *goes into the closet.*)

COUNTESS: My little scheme is certainly bold enough. *(She turns.)* Oh the ribbon! My pretty little ribbon. I almost forgot you! *(She takes it from her chair and rolls it up.)* I'll keep you with me forever. A souvenir of that unhappy child. Oh, Sir, what have you done? And me, what am I doing? *(She secretly puts the ribbon in her bosom.)*

(SUZANNE *returns.*)

SUZANNE: Madam, I was just thinking how perfectly wonderful your plan is. It reconciles everything. Ends everything. Takes in everything. And no matter what happens my marriage is guaranteed!

(COUNTESS *and* SUZANNE *exit.*)

END ACT TWO

ACT THREE

(A room in the castle. COUNT *and* PEDRILLE, *who wears a jacket and boots and holds a sealed satchel, enter.)*

COUNT: *(Briskly)* You understand?

PEDRILLE: Yes, your lordship. *(He leaves.)*

COUNT: *(Calls him back)* Pedrille!

PEDRILLE: Sir?

COUNT: You haven't been seen?

PEDRILLE: Not by a soul.

COUNT: Take the stallion.

PEDRILLE: It's already saddled and waits by the garden gate.

COUNT: Then off you go to Seville.

PEDRILLE: I'll be there in no time.

COUNT: First find out if the page showed up.

PEDRILLE: At the barracks?

COUNT: *(Nods)* And how long he's been there.

PEDRILLE: I understand.

COUNT: Give him his orders and come back as fast as you can.

PEDRILLE: And if he's not there?

COUNT: Come back faster. Now go.

(PEDRILLE *leaves.*)

COUNT: (*Walking around, absorbed in his thoughts*) It was stupid sending Bazile away! I should control my temper. That letter about the Countess, the maid shut up in the closet; her mistress in a state of terror, true or faked? A man jumps out the window and another confesses…. I'm missing something. I've lost control of my own people, to say nothing about the Countess. Could some man really dare to…? Am I losing my mind? She was enjoying herself—suppressed laughter, hardly repressed joy! She cares about her self-respect, but how about my honor? Has Suzanne slyly betrayed my secret? As usual, Figaro keeps me waiting. When he gets here, I must be careful how I approach him.

(FIGARO *appears upstage.*)

COUNT: And trick him into telling me if he knows anything about my interest in Suzanne….

FIGARO: (*Aside*) Here we go.

COUNT: And what, if anything, she's told him.

FIGARO: (*Aside*) How much easier life would be if everyone spoke their thoughts out loud.

COUNT: I'll marry him off to the old woman….

FIGARO: (*Aside*) Bazile might have something to say about that.

COUNT: And leave the young one for me to deal with.

FIGARO: (*Aside*) Try it.

COUNT: (*Turning around*) Who's there?!

FIGARO: (*Approaching*) Me. You wanted to see me?

COUNT: What were you just saying?

FIGARO: I wasn't saying anything.

COUNT: (*Repeating*) "Try it."

FIGARO: Oh that. That was the end of a conversation with one of the servants. "I have another vest in my closet, if you want you can try it."

COUNT: *(Walking up and down)* I see…. Sir, would you mind telling me why you took so long to come after I called?

FIGARO: *(Pretending to arrange his clothes)* I got dirty falling into the vegetable garden. I had to change.

COUNT: It took you an hour?

FIGARO: It takes time.

COUNT: What a world when servants take longer to dress than masters.

FIGARO: In such a world servants don't have servants to help them.

COUNT: *(Furious)* You insolent… Enough. *(Aside)* I won't find out anything if I keep getting angry.

FIGARO: *(Aside)* Until I see what he's up to, I'll play it close to the chest.

COUNT: *(Regaining his composure)* I had been thinking that I would take you to London with me, but on second thought….

FIGARO: You've changed your mind.

COUNT: Since you don't know English.

FIGARO: I know how to say— "God damn."

COUNT: So?

FIGARO: What more do I need?

COUNT: I don't understand.

FIGARO: English is such a wonderful language that a little bit of it goes a long way. God damn is all you need to get anything you want in England. Say you want a chicken. You go into any inn and make like this (*Imitates turning a spit*) to the innkeeper and say "God damn". And he'll bring you a shank of beef and no bread. You want a nice burgundy or a claret, make like this (*Mimes uncorking a bottle*) and "God damn", he'll bring you a beautiful tin pitcher of foaming beer. What more could you ask for? Say you meet one of those lovely creatures who come down the street at a gentle trot, their eyes lowered, elbows pushed back, hips slightly swaying. You blow her a kiss and "God damn", she will slap you so hard you'll fall over. Proof that she understands you perfectly! It is true that the English use a word or two more in conversation, but it doesn't take a genius to see that "God damn" is the very cornerstone of their language. So if Your Lordship had no other reason for leaving me in Spain....

COUNT: (*Aside*) He wants to go; she's told him nothing.

FIGARO: (*Aside*) That she's told me nothing is what I want him to think.

COUNT: Why would Her Ladyship play such a joke on me?

FIGARO: You'd know that better than I.

COUNT: She has everything she wants. I shower her with gifts.

FIGARO: And rain no affection. It is not luxuries she seeks, but necessities.

COUNT: There was a time when you told me everything.

FIGARO: I have not changed.

COUNT: Why is it that everything you say can be taken two ways?

FIGARO: What choice does a careful man have?

COUNT: What an awful way to see yourself.

FIGARO: I see myself as better than as I seem. Can any aristocrat say the same?

COUNT: A hundred times you've set off down the road of fortune, and you've never gotten anywhere.

FIGARO: How could I? That road's always been crowded, what with everybody pushing, elbowing, trampling each other into the ground. Everybody for themselves and to hell with everybody else. That's how things are. And as for me, I wash my hands of the whole mess!

COUNT: You've given up? (Aside) This is a change.

FIGARO: (Aside) Enough parrying. Now I advance!
(To the COUNT) Your Lordship was kind enough to appoint me steward of this castle. It is a handsome position. And if the truth be known, I seek no more advancement and wish only to spend the rest of my life here, with my wife, in the heart of Andalusia....

COUNT: You could take her with you to London.

FIGARO: I'd be gone so often, I'm afraid my marriage would not survive.

COUNT: With your sharp mind you could climb high.

FIGARO: Since when was a keen mind anything but an obstacle to promotion? It is mediocrity and servility which are your keys to the top.

COUNT: You need only to learn from me a little of the art of politics.

FIGARO: I know all I need to know already.

COUNT: Like English? The cornerstone of the language...

FIGARO: Yes, though what I know I take no pride in knowing. And that is—how to pretend to be ignorant when I am not, and how to pretend to know when I am ignorant; how to pretend to hear that which I do

not understand and pretend not to hear that which
I do; how to pretend to be more able than I am; how
to make nothing sound like a great secret; to appear
profound by seeming reclusive, while in fact being a
dull, empty nothing; to perform any role well or badly
as necessary; to send out spies, reward traitors, tamper
with seals, intercept letters, and justify even the most
despicable means under the guise of noble ends. There
you have the world of politics in a nutshell.

COUNT: All you've defined is intrigue.

FIGARO: Politics, intrigue... To me, it's all the same and
you can have it!

COUNT: *(Aside)* He doesn't want to go. Suzanne
betrayed me.

FIGARO: *(Aside)* He gave me an opening and I grabbed
it. *(Aloud)* Is there anything else, Your Lordship?

COUNT: No.

(FIGARO exits.)

COUNT: That man is a puzzle to me. I condescend to
argue with him, and he turns everything upside down.
He squeezes you and then slithers away. Snakes in the
grass, that's what those two are, and they're trying to
get me. Well they deserve each other so let them be
friends or lovers or whatever they like, but by God not
man and wife!

SUZANNE: *(Running in, out of breath)* Excuse me, Your
Lordship...

COUNT: *(Cross)* What is it, young lady?

SUZANNE: You're angry!

COUNT: I assume you want something?

SUZANNE: *(Shyly)* It is Her Ladyship, she feels faint. I
hurried here to borrow Your Lordship's smelling salts.
I'll bring it right back.

COUNT: *(Handing her his vial)* No. Keep it. One day you might need it yourself.

SUZANNE: No, Sir. A woman in my position doesn't have the time to feel faint. We either faint or we don't. Feeling faint is a condition reserved solely for aristocratic women.

COUNT: Even with the fear of losing your fiancée?

SUZANNE: I plan to pay Marceline off with the dowry you promised me.

COUNT: That I promised you?

SUZANNE: *(Lowering her eyes)* That is what I understood, Sir.

COUNT: But with the condition that we "understood" each other.

SUZANNE: *(Eyes down)* Is it not my duty to always "understand" Your Lordship?

COUNT: You little tease, why didn't you make this clear before?

SUZANNE: Is it ever too late to tell the truth?

COUNT: You'll come to the garden tonight?

SUZANNE: I go there every night.

COUNT: What about the way you treated me this morning?

SUZANNE: This morning? What choice did I have with the page behind the armchair?

COUNT: She's right. I forgot about that. Then why have you been so obstinate with Bazile?

SUZANNE: Who needs Bazile? It's none of his business.

COUNT: She's right again. But then what about a certain Figaro, I have reason to believe you've told him everything.

SUZANNE: But of course! I tell him everything—except that which I don't.

COUNT: (Laughing) You charming creature! Then it's a promise? But if you change your mind, understand this: no rendezvous, no dowry; no dowry, no marriage.

SUZANNE: (Curtseying) But also: no marriage, no revival of your ancient custom, Your Lordship.

COUNT: You spunky girl, you have an answer for everything. Upon my honor, I think I'm beginning to moon over her! You better go, your Mistress is waiting for the salts.

SUZANNE: (Laughing, giving him back the vial) Oh, that was just an excuse to see you.

COUNT: (Trying to give her a kiss) Delicious creature!

SUZANNE: (Getting away from him) I have to go.

COUNT: (Aside) She's mine! (Exits)

SUZANNE: I have to tell Her Ladyship.

(FIGARO enters.)

FIGARO: Suzanne! Suzanne! What was all that about?

SUZANNE: I just put him on the wrong scent. (Runs off)

FIGARO: (Following her) What? What are you talking about?

(COUNT returns.)

COUNT: The wrong scent? I see. I was walking headlong into the trap! You little schemers, you shall get yours. The verdict shall be just. Just what you deserve.

(BARTHOLO, MARCELINE enter, dragging back FIGARO. ANTONIO follows them.)

MARCELINE: (To the COUNT) I demand justice! This man has made a promise to me!

FIGARO: A promise? What promise? What are you talking about?

MARCELINE: A promise of marriage.

FIGARO: A written receipt for money she loaned me, nothing more.

MARCELINE: *(To* COUNT*)* Loaned on the condition that you married me.

COUNT: Where is this marriage promise?

BARTHOLO: I have it, Sir.

COUNT: Read it, so we can get this over with.

BARTHOLO: *(Reads)* "I, the undersigned, acknowledge having received from Marceline de Verte-Allure, in the castle of Aguas-Frescas, the sum of two thousand piasters, which sum I shall repay on her demand in that castle; and I will marry her as a sign of my gratitude, etc. etc." signed—Figaro, just Figaro. Sir, ladies and gentlemen, our claim is for the full repayment of this money and the fulfillment of this promise.

COUNT: *(To* FIGARO*)* Any objection to this document as it was read?

FIGARO: Yes, Sir. I object to the malicious, erroneous, or maybe careless way this document has been read. What is written is not "which sum I shall repay...AND I will marry her." but "which sum I shall repay...OR I will marry her." There's a big difference.

COUNT: What is it— "and" or "or"?

BARTHOLO: It's "and"!

FIGARO: It's "or"!

COUNT: I'll read it. *(Takes the paper)*

FIGARO: That's always a good idea, people always see only what they want to see.

COUNT: "I, the undersigned, and so forth…in the castle…and so forth…" Here it is: "which sum I shall repay on her demand in that castle and…or…and…or…" It's hard to read…. There's a blot. I've come across such blots before.

BARTHOLO: I contend that it is the copulative conjunction AND which links the correlative clauses: "I will repay" and "I will marry."

FIGARO: And I contend that it is the alternating conjunction OR which separates the two clauses: "I will repay" and "I will marry". I can be twice as pedantic as he. Talk Latin and I'll talk Greek. I'll bury him.

COUNT: How can we settle this question?

BARTHOLO: Gentlemen, let's not quibble over one little word. For the sake of expediency, we shall concede that it is "or".

FIGARO: Did everyone hear that?

BARTHOLO: So we agree. It was just a minor point. However, let us now examine this document in the following way: (Reads) "Which sum I shall repay on her demand in that castle or I will marry her…." Focus your attention upon the phrase: "On her demand". This "demand", ladies and gentlemen, has already been made, or we would not be here today; hence, as the condition of the demand, ergo: the repayment of the sum, has not been met, the first clause: "which sum I shall repay on her demand" can now be stricken, and we are left with the clause "I will marry her". It's all here in black and white.

FIGARO: On the contrary. My worthy opponent appears to have forgotten his grammar. The phrase "on her demand" is not a derivative of the noun "this demand", but rather of the verb "to demand"; hence this phrase implies an ongoing action, similar to that

expressed by the present participle, "demanding". For
example, in the phrase: "I either silence my criticism
of the king, on demand, or I die. "As my criticism may
be constant, so is the demand for silence. What we
have is a never-changing constant situation. Though
the lady has made her demand, she also continues to
make it, and shall have the right to do so until I repay
her the sum. Yet, this by no means prevents me from
marrying during this time, and should I do so, then
it shall be the later clause: "I will marry her" that is
stricken for reason of common morality, and we are left
with a situation where one is constantly demanding
repayment, and as this is a situation I have experienced
before, I am willing to accept it.

BARTHOLO: Sir, this is sophism!

FIGARO: From you, I take that as a compliment!

COUNT: Enough!

COUNT: Gentlemen, I have heard all I need to. As
lord of this castle, I have had to settle such domestic
disputes many times before. Fortunately, my noble
father trained me in the art of compromise.

MARCELINE: There's compromise and then there's
compromise.

COUNT: Figaro.

FIGARO: Sir.

COUNT: You wish to retain your freedom. And you
shall.

FIGARO: I won?

COUNT: Marceline, you wish to be repaid the sum and
marry this man…. You shall.

FIGARO: I lost?

MARCELINE: How are both things possible?

COUNT: I hereby grant Figaro his freedom to pay the two thousand piasters, or else to marry Marceline within this day. *(He rises.)* Case closed.

ANTONIO: A great verdict!

FIGARO: What's so great about it?

ANTONIO: It'll be great not to have you as my nephew. I can't wait to tell my niece. *(Exits)*

MARCELINE: Now I breathe!

FIGARO: And me—choke!

COUNT: *(Aside)* The pleasure of revenge. I feel better. *(He starts to go.)*

FIGARO: Wait, Sir. I will not marry her!

COUNT: You dare defy the authority of this castle?!

FIGARO: How can I marry her…without my noble parents' consent?

BARTHOLO: What are their names? Show them to us.

FIGARO: Give me a little time. I'm very close to finding them. I've been looking for fifteen years.

BARTHOLO: What an imagination. He's just a foundling.

FIGARO: And not found yet, Doctor. A lost child or perhaps even a stolen one.

COUNT: *(Returning)* Stolen? Lost? Prove it. Or should we just take your word for it?

FIGARO: If the lace clothes, the embroidered shawl, and golden jewels which were with me when I was found by bandits are not sufficient proof of my high birth then the distinctive mark on my arm, which someone took great care to give me, must suffice as the necessary testimony of my being a noble son. Here is the hieroglyphic…. *(Goes to unclothe his right arm)*

MARCELINE: *(Standing up, startled)* A spatula on your right arm!

FIGARO: How did you know?

MARCELINE: Oh God, it's him!

FIGARO: Of course it's me.

BARTHOLO: *(To MARCELINE)* Him who?

MARCELINE: The him who is Emmanuel!

BARTHOLO: *(To FIGARO)* Were you kidnapped by gypsies?

FIGARO: *(Excited)* Near a castle. Good Doctor, if you can, return me to my noble family and fix whatever price you want for this service: mountains of gold mean nothing to my illustrious parents!

BARTHOLO: *(Pointing to MARCELINE)* There is your mother.

FIGARO: Foster mother?

BARTHOLO: Your own mother.

COUNT: His mother!

FIGARO: I don't understand.

MARCELINE: *(Pointing to BARTHOLO)* There is your father.

FIGARO: *(Desolated)* Oh God, pity me!

MARCELINE: Has nature not told you this a thousand times?

FIGARO: Not a word.

COUNT: *(Aside)* His mother! He won't be marrying her!

BARTHOLO: Nor I!

MARCELINE: Nor you? And what about your son? Didn't you promise me....

BARTHOLO: I was a fool. If every little relationship ended in a commitment, everybody'd be married to everybody. (*Pause. He exits.*)

MARCELINE: Or nobody to nobody.

COUNT: This ridiculous turn of events upsets my plans.

(FIGARO *embraces his mother.*)

(ANTONIO *and* SUZANNE *enter.*)

SUZANNE: (*Running in with a purse in her hand*) Stop them! Stop this marriage! I have the money, Her Ladyship gave it to me!

COUNT: (*Aside*) Her Ladyship can go to hell. It's all a conspiracy! (*He leaves.*)

ANTONIO: (*Seeing* FIGARO *embracing* MARCELINE; *to* SUZANNE:) She didn't give it to you for this. Put your money away, girl.

SUZANNE: (*Turns around*) I've seen all I need to, Uncle. Let's go.

FIGARO: (*Stopping her*) Wait. What is it that you see?

SUZANNE: My folly and your shame.

FIGARO: No, it's neither one nor the other.

SUZANNE: (*Angry*) Go ahead and marry her, since you enjoy hugging her so much.

FIGARO: I hug her, but won't marry her.

(SUZANNE *tries to leave;* FIGARO *stops her.*)

SUZANNE: How dare you touch me!

(SUZANNE *slaps* FIGARO *in the face.*)

FIGARO: (*To the others*) So this is love? (*To* SUZANNE) Before running away, please take a good look at this woman.

SUZANNE: I *am* looking at her.

FIGARO: And how do you find her?

SUZANNE: Repulsive.

FIGARO: Jealousy, oh jealousy, God sheds this grace on us.

MARCELINE: *(With open arms)* Sweet Suzanne, come and hug your mother-to-be. This naughty boy who's teasing you is my son.

SUZANNE: *(Runs to her)* You…his mother!

(They embrace, holding each other in their arms for a while.)

ANTONIO: Since when?

FIGARO: Since when do you think?

MARCELINE: *(Excited)* My heart drew me to you, I just misunderstood why.

FIGARO: In my case it was my common sense which spoke to me. All instinct fought against this marriage; though I still never hated you; the fact that I borrowed your money proves that.

MARCELINE: *(Giving him the piece of paper)* Take this and destroy it. What you owe, now keep as your wedding present.

SUZANNE: *(Throws the purse to him)* And this too!

FIGARO: Many thanks.

(He embraces his mother on one side, SUZANNE on the other. Pause)

SUZANNE: What happened to His Lordship?

FIGARO: Let's hurry and find him. If he gets started on some new scheme, we'll be back to square one!

(They run out.)

END ACT THREE

ACT FOUR

(A lobby: COUNTESS *and* SUZANNE*)*

COUNTESS: Do you have a change of clothes for me?

SUZANNE: You won't need any, Madam. The rendezvous is off.

COUNTESS: You've changed your mind?

SUZANNE: It's Figaro. He made me promise not to go.

COUNTESS: You're lying.

SUZANNE: Oh Madam!

COUNTESS: Figaro's not the type to let a dowry escape.

SUZANNE: Then what do you think, Madam?

COUNTESS: That you struck up a new bargain with the Count when you saw how angry he was with you for having told me his plans. I know you by heart! Leave me!

SUZANNE: *(Throwing herself on her knees)* You don't know how much you wrong your Suzanne! How can you even think, after being so kind and giving me the dowry?!

COUNTESS: *(Lifting her up)* There. There…. I didn't know what I was saying. Let me take your place in the garden. My dear, you won't be going there, so you'll be keeping your promise to your husband, while helping me bring home mine.

SUZANNE: You really upset me.

COUNTESS: Sometimes I say the dumbest things. I'm such a scatterbrain. *(She kisses her on the forehead.)* Where exactly is this rendezvous?

SUZANNE: *(Kissing her hand)* All I remember is the word "garden".

COUNTESS: *(Sitting at the table)* Take this pen and let's fix the spot.

SUZANNE: Write to him?

COUNTESS: It must be done.

SUZANNE: Madam, surely, it is you who should....

(SUZANNE sits; COUNTESS dictates.)

COUNTESS: A new ballad with this melody:
Be beautiful tonight
Under the old chestnut tree.
Be beautiful tonight....

SUZANNE: *(Writing)* "...Under the old chestnut tree." Is that it?

COUNTESS: Don't you think it's enough?

SUZANNE: It's fine. *(She folds the letter.)* What about a seal?

COUNTESS: A pin. And that's how we'll have him answer. Write on the back: "Send me back the seal."

SUZANNE: I don't seem to have a pin on me.

COUNTESS: *(Opening her dress)* Take this one. *(The ribbon from her breast falls to the floor.)* My ribbon!

SUZANNE: *(Picking it up)* It's the little theft's, Madam; it was cruel of you to take it from him.

COUNTESS: I certainly wasn't going to let him keep it on his arm. That would've been a pretty sight. Give it here!

SUZANNE: Madam won't wear it anymore. It's been stained with that young man's blood.

COUNTESS: (*Taking it back*) I'll give it to Fanchette, next time I see her.

(FANCHETTE, CHERUBIN *disguised as a girl, a young* SHEPHERDESS, *and other girls carrying bouquets enter.*)

FANCHETTE: Your Ladyship, these village girls have come to give you flowers.

COUNTESS: (*Quickly putting away her ribbon*) How charming. Forgive me, little ones, for not remembering your names. (*Pointing to* CHERUBIN) And who is this cute child who's so shy?

SHEPHERDESS: A cousin of mine, Your Ladyship, who's here just for the wedding.

COUNTESS: She's pretty. Since I can't exactly carry all of these bouquets, let me honor our stranger and take hers. (*Takes the bouquet from* CHERUBIN *and kisses her on the forehead*) She's blushing! (*To* SUZANNE) Suzanne, doesn't she remind you of someone?

SUZANNE: The spitting image, really.

CHERUBIN: (*Aside, his hands on his heart*) How I longed for this kiss!

(*The* COUNT *and* ANTONIO *enter.*)

ANTONIO: I tell you, Sir, he's here. They dressed him at my daughter's. His clothes are still there; here's his hat that I took from his bag.

(ANTONIO *looks at all the girls, recognizes* CHERUBIN, *takes off his woman's bonnet, so his long hair falls. He puts the soldier's hat on his head and says:*)

ANTONIO: By God, here's our soldier!

COUNTESS: (*Recoils*) Oh my God!

SUZANNE: The little devil.

ANTONIO: Like I told you....

COUNT: *(With anger, to* CHERUBIN*)* Why didn't you leave?

CHERUBIN: *(Snatching off his hat)* My Lordship...

COUNT: You'll be punished for your disobedience.

FANCHETTE: *(Thoughtlessly)* Sir, remember when you come to me and want to kiss me how you always say: "If you'll love me, little Fanchette, I'll give you whatever you want." Remember?

COUNT: *(Blushing)* Who? Me?

FANCHETTE: Yes, My Lordship. Now if you were to give me Cherubin to marry, instead of punishing him, I'd love you all you'd want.

COUNTESS: Sir, this child's confession, as innocent as my own, proves two truths: It has never been my wish or my intent to cause you pain, whereas it appears that you have gone to great lengths to inflict me with mine.

ANTONIO: You too, My Lordship? Damn it, I have to set her straight about you just as I did her mother, God rest her soul.... What can you do when little girls become big girls?

COUNT: *(Disconcerted; aside)* There is an evil spirit that seems to be so dead set against me?!

(FIGARO enters.)

FIGARO: Your Lordship, we can't begin the party or the dancing without the girls.

COUNT: You're going to dance? Not after spraining your foot in your fall this morning.

FIGARO: *(Stretching his leg)* It's still a little sore, but it's nothing. *(To the girls)* Come, my beauties, let's go!

COUNT: *(Turning him back)* Lucky for you those vegetable patches were soft.

FIGARO: I guess I was just born lucky.

ANTONIO: *(Turning him back)* But then you curled yourself up as you fell.

FIGARO: A shrewder man would have stopped half way down. *(To the girls)* Are you coming, ladies?

ANTONIO: *(Turning him)* And all this time the little page was galloping to Seville?

FIGARO: Either galloping or strolling there!

COUNT: *(Turning him back)* And you had his orders in your pocket?

FIGARO: *(A little astonished)* Of course, why do you even ask? *(To the girls)* Come on, girls.

ANTONIO: *(Pulling CHERUBIN by the arm)* Yet here is one who claims that my future nephew is a liar!

FIGARO: *(Surprised)* Cherubin!

COUNT: He's been telling us that it was he who jumped into the vegetables.

FIGARO: *(Musing)* Maybe he did, maybe he didn't. How should I know?

COUNT: Two at the same time?

FIGARO: Who knows how many jumped? Could have been a dozen. But what does it matter, no one got hurt. *(To the girls)* Are you coming or not?

COUNT: *(Carried away)* Is this some sort of comedy?!!

(Off—the prelude of a fanfare)

FIGARO: That's the signal for the march. Places, dear one, places! Suzanne, your arm.

(They all run off; CHERUBIN remains with the COUNT and COUNTESS, his head lowered.)

COUNT: *(Watching FIGARO go)* I've never seen a man with so much gall. *(To CHERUBIN)* And you, slyboots,

quit pretending to be ashamed and go get yourself
dressed. But don't let me catch you anywhere near the
party tonight.

COUNTESS: He'll get very bored.

CHERUBIN: (Thoughtlessly) Bored?! One hundred years
of prison could not cool the happiness I now carry
upon my forehead! (He puts on his hat and runs off.)

(COUNTESS fans herself.)

COUNT: What's on his forehead that makes him so
happy?

COUNTESS: (Embarrassed) His...soldier's cap, no doubt.
He's a child with a new toy. (She starts to leave.)

COUNT: You're leaving us, Madam?

COUNTESS: I told you I don't feel well.

COUNT: Stay awhile for your protégé's sake; otherwise,
I'll think you're angry.

COUNTESS: Here come the dancers.

(While the dance and song goes on: SUZANNE, kneeling,
pulls the COUNT's cape and shows him the letter she's
holding. While the COUNT pretends to adjust her bonnet, she
gives him the letter. The COUNT puts it in his breast pocket;
the song is ending, the bride gets up and makes a deep bow.
FIGARO comes to receive her from the COUNT and returns
with her to the other side of the room, near MARCELINE.
During this time another reprise of the fandango is danced.
The COUNT, anxious to read what he has received, moves to
the side of the stage and takes out the paper. But in taking it
out, we see him gesture like he has hurt his finger. He shakes
it, squeezes it, sucks it, while looking at the paper which was
sealed with a pin. While he and FIGARO speak, the orchestra
plays softly.)

COUNT: God damn all women for sticking pins into everything! *(He throws the pin on the floor, then reads the letter while kissing it.)*

FIGARO: *(Who has seen everything; to* MARCELINE *and* SUZANNE*)* A love letter that some girl slipped him. It was sealed with a pin and he got stuck.

(The dance continues. Having read the letter, the COUNT *turns it over and reads the envelope. He searches the floor for the pin, finds it, and attaches it to his sleeve.)*

FIGARO: *(To* SUZANNE *and* MARCELINE*)* Look at him pick up the pin. What a funny man he is!

(During this time, SUZANNE *signals to the* COUNTESS. *The dance ends and the chorus continues.* FIGARO *leads* MARCELINE *to the* COUNT, *takes the bonnet, and the song begins; this is interrupted by cries.)*

VOICES: Stop! You can't all go in there! Stop! Guards! Guards!

COUNT: *(Coming out of his thought)* What is it?

FANCHETTE: *(Entering)* Sir, it's Bazile and it looks like half the town is with him.

MARCELINE: This man is blessed with bad timing.

(BAZILE enters with GRIPE-SOLEIL *and other peasants.)*

BAZILE: Having obeyed His Lordship's order and found thirty-five peasants, all of whom are willing to swear to having been the one who gave me the letter.... I now desire His Lordship to entertain my claims.

COUNT: What are you asking, Bazile?

BAZILE: Only for that which belongs to me—the hand of Marceline.

FIGARO: *(Approaching him)* How long has it been since you've seen the face of a fool?

BAZILE: I see one now.

FIGARO: Since my eyes serve so well as your mirror, study them carefully, for there you will see what's in store for you if you even think about coming near this woman.

MARCELINE: No, let him talk.

BAZILE: Every time I see him, he insults me.

FIGARO: What choice is there?

BAZILE: He tells everyone I'm a fool.

FIGARO: And those I've missed have already met you.

BAZILE: There's not one singer alive who couldn't improve with the help of my talent!

FIGARO: Or one dead.

BAZILE: He's doing it again!

FIGARO: Suffer the truth, you're not important enough for me to suffer your lies.

BAZILE: *(To* MARCELINE*)* Did you or did you not promise me that if after four years you'd not been provided for you would marry me?

MARCELINE: And what was the condition of my promise?

BAZILE: That if you ever found your lost son, I would willingly adopt him.

MARCELINE: He's been found.

BAZILE: Yes? Then if that's all you're worried about....

ALL: *(Pointing to* FIGARO*)* And there he is!

BAZILE: *(Recoiling in fright)* I have seen the devil!

FIGARO: Then you give up your claims to his dear mother?

BAZILE: *(Pointing to* FIGARO*)* If this gentleman is part of the bargain, then I withdraw my offer. *(He goes.)*

FIGARO: *(Laughing)* Ha ha ha ha!

COUNT: Have the contract drawn up. I shall sign it.

ALL: Hurray! Bravo!

COUNT: In an hour.

FIGARO: Why the wait?

COUNT: I wish to rest for a while.

COUNTESS: *(To* SUZANNE*)* This is our chance. Quick, let's change clothes.

SUZANNE: But, Madam…

COUNTESS: Hurry!

(They go. COUNT *has started to leave. The others go;* FIGARO, GRIPE-SOLEIL, *and* MARCELINE *are left.)*

GRIPE-SOLEIL: *(To* FIGARO*)* I'll go set up the fireworks under the big chestnut tree, like I was told.

COUNT: *(Running back)* What fool told you to do that?

FIGARO: Why not?

COUNT: *(Sharply)* Her Ladyship isn't feeling well. She's been…feeling faint. So they'll need to be set up where she can see them from her room. Put them on the terrace.

FIGARO: Hear that, Gripe-Soleil? The terrace.

*(*GRIPE-SOLEIL *leaves.)*

COUNT: *(Aside)* Under the big chestnut! Great! He almost blew up my rendezvous! *(He leaves.)*

FIGARO: All of a sudden he's worried about his wife!

MARCELINE: And yours, Son, I wanted to tell you how wonderful I think she is.

FIGARO: So much so, Mother, that should I ever find her unfaithful to me I pardon her in advance.

MARCELINE: But jealousy…

FIGARO: ...is either the silly child of pride or the sickness of a fool. One more hour to wait!

(FIGARO *turns and sees* FANCHETTE, *who is searching for someone.*)

FIGARO: Look, we have an eavesdropper!

FANCHETTE: I was looking for someone.

FIGARO: So young and already lying! You little flirt, you know he's not in here.

FANCHETTE: Who?

FIGARO: Cherubin.

FANCHETTE: I'm not looking for him; I know where he is. It's my cousin, Suzanne.

FIGARO: And what do you want with her?

FANCHETTE: It's this pin, I'm supposed to return it to her.

FIGARO: A pin! A pin! Where'd you get it? So young and already plying your trade.... (*Stops himself and speaks in a low voice*) It's very sweet of you to have tried to find her, Fanchette. You've been very helpful.

FANCHETTE: How come you're angry? I better go.

FIGARO: (*Stopping her*) No, no, I was joking. I know all about the pin, it's the one His Lordship gave you to give to Suzanne. It was the seal for that letter he had. Am I right?

FANCHETTE: Yes. If you already knew, why'd you ask me?

FIGARO: I'd be amused to know how His Lordship came to give you this job.

FANCHETTE: (*Naively*) It was just like you said: "Little Fanchette, take this pin to your beautiful cousin and tell her it is the seal of the big chestnut tree."

FIGARO: "The big..."?

FANCHETTE: Chestnut tree. And then he said: "Make sure no one sees you."

FIGARO: He should be obeyed, Cousin. Fortunately, no one has seen you. Go and finish the job, but tell Suzanne only what His Lordship has told you to say.

FANCHETTE: Why should I tell her anything else? What do you take me for—a child? *(She leaves, skipping.)*

FIGARO: Well, Mother?

MARCELINE: Well, Son?

FIGARO: *(Like he's choking)* That just goes to prove... some things never change.

MARCELINE: What things?

FIGARO: *(Hands on his chest)* The things that I've just learned. It's like I've been shot.

MARCELINE: *(Laughing)* Your confidence is like a balloon, one pin pops it!

FIGARO: *(Angry)* But that pin, Mother, was the one he picked up!

MARCELINE: Jealousy! "Oh, Mother, should Suzanne ever be unfaithful to me, I hereby pardon her in advance!"

FIGARO: Revenge is the first right of marriage!

MARCELINE: But Son, how do you know what she'll say to him? Or what she'll do with him?

FIGARO: I've got a good idea. I know where the rendezvous is! *(He exits.)*

MARCELINE: And so do I! *(She exits.)*

END ACT FOUR

ACT FIVE

(A group of chestnut trees in a garden; two pavilions are at left and right; the background is a landscaped clearing; a garden seat downstage. The stage is dark.)

(FANCHETTE enters, alone, holding two biscuits and an orange in one hand, a lit paper lantern in the other.)

FANCHETTE: He said, the pavilion to the left. There it is. But what if my little partner doesn't show up?... Those horrible people in the kitchen didn't even want to give me an orange and two biscuits! Who are they for, Miss? Oh, Sir, they are for someone. Ah! We know who! So what if they do?! Just because he has to stay out of His Lordship's sight, doesn't mean he has to starve to death. In the end it cost me a wet kiss on the cheek. But who knows, maybe he'll pay me back!

(FANCHETTE sees FIGARO, who comes and looks at her closely. She cries out:)

FANCHETTE: Ah! *(And runs away, hiding in the left pavilion)*

(FIGARO wears a coat over his shoulders, and a large hat turned down. BAZILE, ANTONIO, BARTHOLO, GRIPE-SOLEIL, and workmen enter.)

FIGARO: *(To himself)* It's Fanchette! *(He fiercely surveys the others as they arrive.)* Good evening, gentlemen. Is everyone here?

BAZILE: Everyone you asked to come.

FIGARO: About what time is it?

ANTONIO: (*Looking up*) The moon should be up by now.

BARTHOLO: What dark plot are you planning now? He has the look of a conspirator!

FIGARO: It is here, under these chestnuts, that we must sing our praises to my honest bride and our honest lord who has planned his own festivities for tonight.

BAZILE: Ah! I know what this is about. Quick, let's get out of sight. Trust me: It's a question of a rendezvous. I'll tell you about it later.

FIGARO: Now come, when I call, all of you. And if the show you'll see isn't a good one, you can take it out on me.

BAZILE: (*Aside*) The Count and his Suzanne deserve anything they get for arranging this without me.

FIGARO: (*To the servants*) And you, little devils, when I give the order I better see this sky light up, or by my life—which soon may not be worth much—if I ever get my hands on you…. (*He grabs the arm of* GRIPE-SOLEIL.)

GRIPE-SOLEIL: (*Howling and crying*) Ah! Ah! That hurts! Stop it!

BAZILE: (*As he goes*) May the Heavens bring you happiness, Mister Bridegroom!

(*They all leave, except for* FIGARO.)

FIGARO: (*Walking in the dark; he speaks with somber tones.*) O woman! woman! woman! You weak deceitful creature. As each beast must be true to its nature, is it the nature of the beast, woman, to deceive?… After flatly refusing, in the presence of her mistress, when I urged it, after giving me her word, then while giving me her word, then while giving me her hand!… He's laughing while he reads; what a monster and me, what a fool!… No, Sir, you will not have her…you will not

have her. Because you're a lord you think you're God's
gift to the world!...
Nobility, wealth, position; because of these you think
you can do as you want. But how have you earned any
of this? You suffered a little when you were born, that's
about it. Inside, you're nothing much. But goddamnit,
the same can't be said for me! Thrown alone into the
black sea of humanity, I survived on more wit and
cunning than has been used to rule all of Spain for the
past one hundred years! And you want to tangle with
me!... Someone's coming!... It's her.... *(Listens)* It's
nobody. The night is as dark as the devil. Already I'm
cast in the role of the ridiculous husband and I haven't
even finished being married! *(Sits on the bench)* Mine
has been a bizarre destiny. Son of I didn't know who,
kidnapped by bandits, taught their ways; I become
disgusted and wish only to pursue an honest trade; but
who will let me? I study chemistry, pharmacy, surgery,
and with the sponsorship of a great nobleman climb
up the ladder of success to the prized position of cow
doctor! I grow tired of causing pain in sick animals to
say nothing about constantly cleaning off my boots,
so I throw myself headlong into the world of theater;
I might as well have gone swimming carrying a bag
of rocks. I piece together a comedy based upon a tale
out of *The Arabian Nights.* An inoffensive choice, I felt,
for a Spanish writer. I was wrong: An envoy, from
God knows where, complains that I have offended in
my verse the holy religion of Mohammed, the country
of Persia, a part of some peninsula of the Indies, the
whole of Egypt, and the kingdoms of Barca, Tripoli,
Tunis, Algeria, and Morocco. And so there goes my
little comedy, burned alive to please some illiterate
Arab princes who want nothing better than to stab
us Spaniards in the back, if we'd ever give them the
chance; my harmless little play, sacrificed in the name
of good trade relations! —Fact: When the world is

unable to break a man's spirit, it next tries to break his
bones! So I'm becoming thin, my cheeks are sunken,
I have no money to pay the rent, at night I wait for
the knock at the door and the arrival of the marshal
from debtor's prison; I try to steady myself. Aware
that economics is a popular subject of the day, and
believing that my great poverty has made me an
expert on the importance of being wealthy, I write an
essay on the value of wealth and its net effects. Next
I experience from the bottom of a carriage a castle's
drawbridge being lowered for me and the loss of all
hope of liberty! *(He rises.)* How I would love to get
my hands on one of those simpering officials who
blindly impose decrees, ignorant of the suffering they
cause; if I could only get to him after some scandal
has touched him, and once his star has fallen, then I
would say...little books take on big importance only
when they are banned! Without the right to criticism,
praise itself becomes suspect! Only petty minds fear
petty works! *(He sits again.)* Tired of paying my room
and board, they throw me back into the street. But
freedom, though delicious, won't fill the stomach, so
I take up my pen once again. Inquiring after a worthy
subject to write about, I'm told that there's been a
political thaw; that products once strictly controlled
are now freely and openly on sale; and that this new
open spirit extends to the press as well. Provided I do
not write about the state, religion, politics, morality,
important men, important organizations, operatic or
other theatrical productions, or anyone or anything
that may have some standing in the community, I am
free to print what I please—provided it passes two
or three censors. Set to make the most of this new-
found liberty, I announce plans for a new magazine;
and not wanting to step on anyone's toes, I call it *The
About Nothing Journal.* Christ! In no time, a thousand
official hacks descend upon me, close me down, and

brand me an experimentalist. Once again, I'm out of
work. Desperation almost gets the better of me, when
someone thinks to give me a job. Unfortunately, I am
qualified for it, it requires an aptitude for numbers,
so they give it to a dancer. Nothing remains but to
steal. So I set up a floating card game. Now that's the
life: dining out, rubbing shoulders with the rich, who
are nice enough to open their homes to my game,
while taking only three quarters of the profits. My
losses I could have recouped—especially since I was
beginning to learn that to make money requires not
intelligence but the right attitude: the less you seem to
care about it, the easier it is to get. But as everyone else
is always cheating, and I remain honest, I'm doomed
to bankruptcy. After this blow, I decide to renounce
the world and on a cliff watch the twenty fathoms of
water that's about to separate me from it, when God,
oh dear God, directs me back to my former calling,
and with razor and razor strap I take my shaving from
city to city, leaving ambition to any fool who wishes
to feed on it, and my pride on some road side, it being
too great a burden to drag along with me. At last,
I don't have a care in the world. In Seville, I meet a
noble lord. He recognizes me. I get him married; and
in return for my help in getting him his wife, he now
helps himself to mine! A world of intrigue and dark
clouds! In life, you hang on by your fingertips: About
to marry my mother, my parents arrive out of the blue.
(He rises.) We debate: It's you; it's him; it's me; no, it
can't be! What can't be, usually is. (Falls into his seat)
What a bizarre turn of events! Why does everything
always happen to me? Why one thing and not another
thing? What have I done to deserve this life? Nobody
asked me if I wanted to come into this world, and now
nobody asks me about what happens to me while I'm
here. My life has known much happiness, but this
happiness, did I actually feel it or only show it? And

who is this `I' that so preoccupies me? It is but a mass
of unknown parts: a puny mindless being, a small
frisky animal, a young man in search of pleasure,
with a taste for anything, while trying everything just
to earn enough to live; master here, servant there,
depending on the day. Ambitious out of vanity, hard
working when necessary, lazy whenever possible.
Fast talker when in trouble, poet when time permits,
musician when occasion demands, lover on and off.
I have seen everything, done everything, exhausted
everything. Every illusion has been shattered and I am
disillusioned! Disillusioned! Disillusioned! Suzanne!
Suzanne! Suzanne! The torture you put me through. I
hear steps...someone's coming. The moment has come.
(He moves far stage right.)

*(*COUNTESS*, dressed as* SUZANNE*;* SUZANNE*, dressed as the*
COUNTESS*; and* MARCELINE *enter.)*

SUZANNE: *(Low, to* COUNTESS*)* Marceline told me Figaro
would be here.

MARCELINE: And so he is; lower your voice.

SUZANNE: Let's begin.

MARCELINE: I don't want to miss a word; I'll hide in the
pavilion. *(She hides where* FANCHETTE *is hiding.)*

SUZANNE: *(Loudly)* Madam, your hands are shaking!
Are you cold?

COUNTESS: *(Loudly)* The night is damp, I'm going to
bed.

SUZANNE: If Your Ladyship doesn't need me, I think I'll
take some air under these trees.

COUNTESS: This air will cover you with dew.

SUZANNE: I'm prepared for that.

FIGARO: *(Aside)* Oh yes. The "dew"!

(SUZANNE *moves close to the wings, on the opposite side of the stage from* FIGARO.)

(CHERUBIN *enters, dressed as an officer. He enters singing the reprise of a ballad.*)

CHERUBIN: *(Gaily)* La, la, la, etc. etc. "She's too far above me, to love me!"

COUNTESS: *(Aside)* The little page!

CHERUBIN: *(Stops)* I'm not alone. Quick, to my hiding place, where little Fanchette awaits... It's a woman!

COUNTESS: *(Listening)* Oh good God!

CHERUBIN: *(Looking from a distance, into the darkness)* Do my eyes deceive me? By the silhouette of that hat, it looks like Suzanne.

COUNTESS: *(Aside)* If the Count were to come now!

(COUNT *appears in the distance.* CHERUBIN *approaches and takes the* COUNTESS's *hand. She tries to hide her face.*)

CHERUBIN: No, I was right, it is Suzanne. I could never mistake the sweet softness of this hand for another's. *(He tries to kiss the back of her hand; she pulls it away.)*

COUNTESS: *(Quickly)* Go away!

CHERUBIN: Has pity brought you here to where I have been hiding?

COUNTESS: Figaro's coming.

COUNT: *(Advancing; aside)* Is that Suzanne?

CHERUBIN: *(To* COUNTESS) It's not Figaro I'm worried about, because it's not him you're here to meet.

COUNTESS: Who then?

COUNT: *(Aside)* She's with someone.

CHERUBIN: It's His Lordship, you flirt. Don't forget I was behind the chair this morning.

COUNT: *(Aside, furious)* It's that damn page again!

FIGARO: *(Aside)* And they say it's not nice to eavesdrop!

SUZANNE: *(Aside)* Who's he calling a flirt?

COUNTESS: *(To* CHERUBIN*)* Let me go!

CHERUBIN: I will but it will cost you.

COUNTESS: *(Horrified)* Are you insane?

CHERUBIN: *(With passion)* Twenty kisses for you and then a hundred more for your beautiful mistress.

COUNTESS: You wouldn't dare.

CHERUBIN: Oh yes, I would!

FIGARO: *(Aside)* I'll kill him!

SUZANNE: *(Aside)* Bold for a page!

*(*CHERUBIN *tries to embrace the* COUNTESS; *the* COUNT *puts himself between the two and receives the kiss.)*

COUNTESS: *(Drawing back)* Oh my God!

FIGARO: *(Aside; having heard the kiss)* And I thought I was marrying a sweet girl! *(He listens.)*

CHERUBIN: *(Aside, fumbling with the* COUNT*'s clothes)* It's His Lordship! *(He runs to the pavilion where* FANCHETTE *and* MARCELINE *are hiding.)*

FIGARO: *(Approaching)* Enough is enough...

COUNT: *(Thinking he is speaking to* CHERUBIN*)* That's your last kiss.... *(Slaps him, thinking it is* CHERUBIN*)*

FIGARO: Ah!

COUNT: And that's what it costs!

FIGARO: *(Aside, withdrawing, rubbing his cheek)* Maybe eavesdropping isn't the solution.

SUZANNE: *(Laughing loudly from the other side)* Ha ha ha ha!

COUNT: *(To the* COUNTESS, *whom he takes to be* SUZANNE*)*
I don't know what to make of that page; the harder you
slap him the louder he laughs.

FIGARO: *(Aside)* He wouldn't if he'd gotten it.

COUNT: Everywhere I look, he crawls out.... But no
more of him; it'll only poison my pleasure in having
found you here.

COUNTESS: *(Imitating* SUZANNE's *voice)* Did you expect
to?

COUNT: There was your clever note. *(Takes her hand)*
You're trembling.

COUNTESS: I was frightened.

COUNT: It wasn't to deprive you of kisses that I asked
you here. *(He kisses her.)*

COUNTESS: What liberties!

FIGARO: *(Aside)* The whore!

SUZANNE: *(Aside)* How nice!

COUNT: *(Taking his wife's hand)* Such skin, had the
Countess a hand half so soft.

COUNTESS: *(Aside)* What prejudice!

COUNT: Or arms as firm and round; or fingers as
graceful and as mischievous.

COUNTESS: *(In* SUZANNE's *voice)* Don't you love her?

COUNT: What is love but a book you keep adding
chapters to? Pleasure, I believe, is more to the point.

COUNTESS: So you don't love her anymore?

COUNT: I love her very much; but three years of
marriage has made it all so respectable!

COUNTESS: What do you want from her?

COUNT: *(Caressing her)* What I find in you, my
beauty....

COUNTESS: No, tell me.

COUNT: I don't know; less predictability perhaps.
That certain I-don't-know-what which is charming.
A refusal now and then. A wife thinks that to love is
enough—that is, she who loves us to begin with—and
once the foundation of love is in place…. She just loves
and loves and what had been mysterious becomes
common and what had been exciting is now obliging,
until you wake up one morning to find yourself full,
but not satisfied.

COUNTESS: *(Aside)* I'm learning.

COUNT: In truth, Suzanne, I've often thought that if we
keep seeking pleasure apart from our wives, it's only
because our wives have not studied the art of keeping
themselves interesting. Love needs constantly to be
revived.

COUNTESS: *(Stung)* So it's all up to the wife?

COUNT: *(Laughing)* You want the husband to do
everything? You want to change nature? Our task is to
get them, theirs….

COUNTESS: Theirs…?

COUNT: To keep us. Too often that's forgotten.

COUNTESS: I won't forget it. I won't.

COUNT: Nor I.

FIGARO: *(Aside)* Nor I.

SUZANNE: *(Aside)* Nor I.

COUNT: *(Taking his wife's hand)* There's an echo here.
Speak softer. But don't worry your pretty little head,
none of what I say can concern you, love has made
you too alive. *(He kisses her hand.)* Here is the gold to
repurchase the right—which I no longer have—to
enjoy the delicious moment which you have granted

me. But as such a thing is priceless, take also this diamond to wear as a token of our love.

COUNTESS: *(With reverence)* Suzanne accepts everything.

FIGARO: *(Aside)* She would make the devil blush.

SUZANNE: *(Aside)* Another wedding present!

COUNT: *(Aside)* She's mercenary; that's encouraging.

COUNTESS: *(Looking back)* I see torches.

COUNT: For your wedding. Let's go into one of these pavilions, until they pass.

COUNTESS: It's dark in there.

COUNT: We won't be reading.

FIGARO: *(Aside)* She's going with him. I knew she would. *(He comes forward.)*

COUNT: *(Raising his voice and turning around)* Who goes there?

FIGARO: *(Angered)* Going?! I'm coming!

COUNT: *(Whispering to* COUNTESS*)* It's Figaro! *(He runs away.)*

COUNTESS: Wait for me!

(COUNTESS *enters the pavilion, stage right, while the* COUNT *is lost in the woods upstage.* FIGARO, *in the darkness, tries to see where they've gone.)*

FIGARO: I don't hear anything now. They've gone in; and I'm out here. *(With forced calm)* You, other foolish husbands, who live day to day with suspicion, why don't you follow my example. I didn't waste a day before checking on my wife, and now after listening to her, not to have a single doubt—that's a good feeling…. It's always nice to know where you stand. *(He paces. Yells:)* I've got them cornered!!!

SUZANNE: *(Who has advanced softly in the darkness; aside)* You will pay for these suspicions. *(In the* COUNTESS' *voice)* Who's there?

FIGARO: "Who's there?" A man who wishes he'd never been born.

SUZANNE: Oh! It's Figaro!

FIGARO: *(Looking at her, and saying quickly)* Your Ladyship!

SUZANNE: Not so loud.

FIGARO: *(Loudly)* Madam, you are Heaven sent! Guess where His Lordship is?

SUZANNE: Why should I care where that ungrateful man is? Tell me…

FIGARO: *(Loudly)* And Suzanne, my bride, guess where she is?

SUZANNE: Not so loud!

FIGARO: *(Very loud)* Our Suzanne, whom everyone thinks is so innocent and sweet! They're both in there. I'll call them out.

SUZANNE: *(Holding her hand over her mouth, to disguise her voice)* Don't call them.

FIGARO: *(Aside)* It's Suzanne!

SUZANNE: You look upset.

FIGARO: *(Aside)* Traitor, it's all a trap!

SUZANNE: Figaro, I must have my revenge.

FIGARO: Funny, you too? I was thinking the same thing.

SUZANNE: Would I be a woman if I didn't? But men know a hundred cunning ways to….

FIGARO: *(Confident)* Pardon me for disagreeing, Your Ladyship. But when it comes to revenge, a man must always bow to a woman. They are more practiced.

SUZANNE: *(Aside)* He's asking for it.

FIGARO: *(On his knees, with comic fervor)* Oh Madam, I love you. Consider the place, the circumstance, and allow your anger to forgive the awkwardness of my heart's confession!

SUZANNE: *(Aside)* My hand's itching.

FIGARO: My heart's racing. Your hand, Madam?

SUZANNE: *(In her own voice)* There it is! *(She slaps him.)*

FIGARO: Ah! Blessed Virgin, what a slap!

SUZANNE: You think that was something, try this!

(SUZANNE slaps FIGARO again.)

FIGARO: Ah! Where did that come from? What is this, national Slap Figaro Day?

SUZANNE: *(Hitting him with each phrase)* Where did that come from? It came from me—Suzanne! And here's another one for being suspicious of me! And another one for your revenge! And one for your treachery! And here's one for everything you thought about doing but didn't have the chance to do! And one for everything you hadn't thought about doing yet, but might have, given the time!

FIGARO: Stop! How could I not have recognized my bride's pretty voice?

SUZANNE: *(Laughing)* You recognized me? Oh, I hate you!

FIGARO: First you hit, then you hate, with men it's usually the other way around. But tell me, what foolishness are you up to?

SUZANNE: Ah, it's you who has been foolish enough to walk into a trap set for another! It's not our fault if in trying to catch one fox, we end up snaring two.

FIGARO: Who caught the other one?

SUZANNE: His wife.

FIGARO: His wife?

SUZANNE: His wife.

FIGARO: (*Wildly, falls on his knees*) Ah. Figaro! Go hang yourself! Why didn't you figure that out?

SUZANNE: (*Laughing*) Oh, the poor Count! All the trouble he's gone to….

FIGARO: To conquer his wife!

(COUNT *enters from the back of the stage, and turns to the pavilion, stage right.*)

COUNT: (*To himself*) I've looked everywhere in the woods; maybe she went in here.

SUZANNE: (*To* FIGARO, *whispering*) It's him.

COUNT: (*Opening the pavilion door*) Suzanne, is that you?

FIGARO: Do we dare? (*He kisses her hand.*)

COUNT: (*Turning around*) A man on his knees in front of the Countess! And me, without a sword! (*Comes forward*)

FIGARO: (*Standing suddenly and disguising his voice*) How unfortunate, Your Ladyship, that our usual meeting place was invaded by the wedding party.

COUNT: (*Aside*) It's the man from the closet! (*Hits his forehead*)

FIGARO: (*Continuing*) But let us not allow this inconvenience to delay our pleasure.

COUNT: (*Aside*) I'll kill them. Both of them!

FIGARO: (*Guiding her to the pavilion*) Let's make up for the time lost when I was forced to jump out the window.

COUNT: (*Aside*) The truth at last!

SUZANNE: *(Near the pavilion)* Before we go in, see if we've been followed.

(FIGARO kisses her.)

COUNT: *(Crying out)* Revenge!!!!!

(SUZANNE runs into the pavilion where CHERUBIN, FANCHETTE, and MARCELINE are hiding.)

(The COUNT seizes FIGARO by the arm.)

FIGARO: *(With excessive dread)* Oh God! It is my master!

COUNT: *(Recognizing him)* Ah! Villain, it's you! Help!

(PEDRILLE enters.)

PEDRILLE: There you are, Sir, I've been looking everywhere for you.

COUNT: It's Pedrille, good. Where is everybody?

PEDRILLE: I don't know. I just arrived from Seville. I have news.

COUNT: Yell! Yell!

PEDRILLE: Has his Lordship lost his hearing?

COUNT: Yell!

PEDRILLE: *(Yelling)* There was no sign of the page! Here are his orders!

COUNT: *(Pushing him back)* What the hell are you doing?

PEDRILLE: Your Lordship told me to yell.

COUNT: *(Still holding FIGARO)* For help! For help! Hello?! Anybody hear me?! I need help!

(ANTONIO, BARTHOLO, BAZILE, GRIPE-SOLEIL, and the rest of the wedding party run in with torches.)

COUNT: *(Pointing to the pavilion.)* Pedrille, guard the entrance.

(PEDRILLE moves to the pavilion)

BAZILE: *(Whispers to* FIGARO*)* You caught him with Suzanne?

COUNT: *(Pointing to* FIGARO*)* And the rest of you, surround this man; anyone who lets him escape, pays with his life.

BAZILE: Oh! Oh!

COUNT: *(Furious)* Quiet! *(To* FIGARO, *in an icy tone)* Sir, will you answer my questions?

FIGARO: *(Coldly)* What choice do I have? You're in command here, of everything but yourself.

COUNT: *(Controlling himself)* Would you mind telling us who the lady is that you brought to this pavilion?

FIGARO: *(Maliciously, he points to the other one.)* That one there?

COUNT: *(Sharply)* No, that one there!

FIGARO: *(Coolly)* Oh. That's different. A young lady who honors me with her kindness.

BAZILE: *(Shocked)* Ah! Ah!

COUNT: *(To* FIGARO*)* And this young lady, is she involved with anyone else that you can think of?

FIGARO: *(Coolly)* I know a great lord who has been involved with her for some time; I don't know if it's because he's neglected her, or whether she just finds me more interesting, but I do know that at least for today I was her choice.

COUNT: *(Quickly)* Her choice… *(Controlling himself)* At least he's honest. *(With furor)* Now we will make this dishonor public, as we shall the punishment! *(He enters the pavilion.)*

ANTONIO: It's only fair.

GRIPE-SOLEIL: *(To* FIGARO*)* Who took whose wife?

FIGARO: *(Laughing)* Neither has had that particular pleasure.

COUNT: *(In the pavilion, dragging someone out whom we cannot see)* Give up, Madam, you've lost! Your hour has come! *(Goes on without looking at the person)* Lucky for you that you were caught before....

FIGARO: *(Crying out)* Cherubin!

COUNT: My page?

BAZILE: Ah! Ah!

COUNT: *(Beside himself)* It's always him! *(To* CHERUBIN*)* What were you doing in there?

CHERUBIN: Hiding from you, as you told me to do.

PEDRILLE: For this I ruined a good horse!

COUNT: Antonio, you go in there; let this vile creature who has so dishonored me be brought to justice!

BARTHOLO: Is it your wife you're looking for?

*(*ANTONIO *goes in.)*

COUNT: What you will see, gentlemen, is that the page was not alone.

CHERUBIN: *(Timidly)* I was depressed, I just wanted some company.

ANTONIO: *(Dragging someone out by the arm)* Come on, Madam, there's no use fighting, we all knew you were in there.

FIGARO: *(Crying out)* My little cousin!

BAZILE: Ah! Ah!

COUNT: FANCHETTE!

ANTONIO: *(Turning around and crying out)* Ah! For Christ's sake, Sir, did you have to choose me to be the one to show to the world what kind of daughter I have!

COUNT: *(Outraged)* How did I know she was in there? *(He starts to enter.)*

BARTHOLO: Permit me, Your Lordship. There appears to be some confusion, and I'm more in control of myself. *(Speaking to someone as he brings her out)* Don't be scared, Madam, I promise you won't be hurt. *(Turns and cries out)* Marceline!

BAZILE: Ah! Ah!

COUNT: *(Outraged)* To hell with them, it's the Countess, I....

(SUZANNE enters with a fan over her face.)

COUNT: Ah! Here she is! *(He grabs her violently by the arm.)* Tell me, gentlemen, what do you think I should do to this odious woman?

(SUZANNE falls on her knees, head lowered.)

COUNT: Never! Never!

(FIGARO falls to his knees, on the other side.)

COUNT: Never! Never!

(Everyone falls on their knees.)

COUNT: Not if there were a hundred of you!

(COUNTESS enters from the other pavilion.)

COUNTESS: *(Falling on her knees)* What about one of me?

COUNT: *(Seeing the COUNTESS and SUZANNE)* Ah! Who is this?

BARTHOLO: From here, it looks like your wife.

COUNT: *(Tries to bring her to her feet)* It was you, Countess? *(In a supplicating tone)* I can only beg for your pardon....

COUNTESS: *(Laughing)* You'd say "Never! Never!" if you were in my place. But for the third time today, I forgive you.

SUZANNE: *(Rising)* Me too.

MARCELINE: *(Rising)* Me too.

FIGARO: *(Rising)* Me too. There's an echo here.

(All rise.)

COUNT: *(To SUZANNE)* The note with the pin?

SUZANNE: Her Ladyship's idea.

COUNT: I've owed you this far too long. *(Kisses the COUNTESS' hand)*

COUNTESS: To each—what they own. *(She gives the purse to FIGARO and the diamond to SUZANNE.)*

SUZANNE: *(To FIGARO)* Another dowry.

FIGARO: *(Hitting the purse with his hand)* And of the three, this one took the most sweat.

SUZANNE: Like our marriage.

GRIPE-SOLEIL: And the marriage garter, can I have it?

COUNTESS: *(Pulls the ribbon she had guarded so long in her bosom and throws it on the ground)* The garter? I found it in her clothes. There.

(The men of the wedding party go to pick it up; CHERUBIN is the quickest and grabs it.)

CHERUBIN: It's mine! And I'll fight anyone who tries to get it away from me!

COUNT: *(Laughing, to CHERUBIN)* For someone so touchy, I wonder how you like being slapped?

CHERUBIN: *(Recoiling and drawing his sword halfway)* A slap? What slap?

FIGARO: *(With mock anger)* I'm the one who got the slap. See how great men dispense justice?!

COUNT: *(Laughing)* You?! Ha ha ha, what do you think about that, my love?

COUNTESS: *(Preoccupied, comes back to the present and says with feeling)* Yes, my dear Count, forever without distraction, I assure you.

FIGARO: When I was poor, people despised me; when I showed a little intelligence, the hate grew. But now with a pretty wife and a fortune....

BARTHOLO: ...everybody will like you?

FIGARO: You think it's possible?

BARTHOLO: I doubt it. I know them.

FIGARO: *(Looking at the audience)* I don't see why they wouldn't. Except for having a pretty wife and a fortune, they're just like me.

END ACT FIVE

END OF PLAY

CPSIA information can be obtained
at www.ICGtesting.com
Printed in the USA
LVHW041706250719
625347LV00014B/627/P

9 780881 450996